Interrogation

A Complete Manual

Neither the author nor the publisher assumes any responsibility for the use of misuse of information contained in this book. It is sold for entertainment purposes only! Be Warned!

INTERROGATION: A COMPLETE MANUAL

by Burt Rapp

Loompanics Unlimited
Port Townsend, Washington

INTERROGATION: A Complete Manual
©1987 by Loompanics Unlimited
All Rights Reserved
Printed in USA

Published by:
Loompanics Unlimited
PO Box 1197
Port Townsend, WA 98368

ISBN 0-915179-59-8
Library of Congress Catalog
  Card Number 87-81101

TABLE OF CONTENTS

INTRODUCTION

Interrogation has gone through many phases, because of its usefulness in criminal investigation, counter-espionage, and even suppression of religious heresy. In ancient times, the simple and obvious method for dealing with reluctant confessors was torture. During the Nineteenth and Twentieth Centuries, we've seen a proliferation of interrogation techniques, and many refinements in the methods. The emphasis now is not on physical torture, although this is still available as a last resort, but on psychological persuasion and coercion.

Interrogators have been very inventive. Many workers in the field have made intense efforts trying to use scientific methods to extract information. Some examples are "truth serum," the "polygraph," and the "voice stress analyzer." Unfortunately, all of these methods have had their problems, and none has lived up to the promises of their originators and boosters.

While in many countries the techniques of interrogation are straightforward, in the Soviet Union and the United States there have been some radical departures from traditional methods because of special local conditions.

1

The Soviets brought psychological interrogation to a high polish, using Pavlovian methods of conditioning and sensory deprivation. With few, if any, restrictions on the behavior of the secret police, they have had room to develop and openly apply methods that would be banned in many Western countries.

In the United States, where there have been judicial restrictions on police interrogation methods during the last two decades (Miranda, Escobedo, etc.), interrogation has become much more subtle, with emphasis on refined psychological methods that can't be used to discredit a confession in court. This is the psychological equivalent of beating a suspect with a wet towel so as not to leave marks. The "third degree" has largely been abandoned, with occasional conspicuous exceptions.

Overlaying all of this has been a mass of propaganda. During WWII, and the cold war which followed, there have been accusations of brutality and coercive methods applied to the enemy's police. Many of these were based on nuggets of fact, but the main effect of the propaganda has been to promote an impression that the police of the other side are sadistic brutes, and the democratic police are solicitous of the rights of the accused. This is a simplified view of events, and the raw fact is that there is a repertoire of methods used by police everywhere, regardless of ideology. At the same time, we must not make the error of thinking that there aren't any differences between the various powers involved. People tend to get a fairer deal from the police in the West, although at the price of many obviously guilty people going free.

Any study of interrogation, especially that of the differences between the methods used by the Western police and counter-espionage agencies and

2

those of the Eastern Bloc, is inevitably impeded by ideologies of the parties involved. Many are ready to believe the worst about the Soviets and to completely disregard any shortcomings of our side. Arriving at a balanced view is extraordinarily difficult because of the ideological and emotional overtones accruing to the simple facts.

Despite the similarities in methods between the police forces of the democratic and totalitarian regimes, their ends are different in certain significant ways. One net result that's easy to see is that the Eastern Bloc countries have large and elaborate border guard forces, using physical fortifications such as the "Berlin Wall," to keep their populations in. By contrast, the United States has the problem of guarding a very porous frontier to keep illegal immigrants out.

PRACTICAL NOTES

It's important to distinguish at the outset between an "interrogation" and an "interview." An interview is a talk with someone whom we can call a "friendly witness," someone who is willing to help and who presumably has no reason for untruthfulness. The person may be a witness to a crime, or a crime victim. He or she may be a relative or neighbor of the accused, although this sometimes brings in problems with bias and an effort to protect the accused. Generally, the interview is an effort to elicit accurate information from a nominally cooperative person.

An interrogation is a talk with the accused or a co-conspirator. The subject nominally has something to conceal. An attitude of outward cooperation may be simply a tactic for masking deception.

3

There isn't a sharp distinction between situations which call for an interview and those which signify an interrogation. This is because in many instances the interviewee's role may not be clear. A businessman who reports arson may have set the fire himself to collect the insurance. A "rape victim" may be exaggerating or confabulating in a spirit of revenge. In cases of mutual combat, the accounts from each side will often differ greatly, making it difficult to decide who was the aggressor, unless there's third-party testimony. Even this can be tainted if the third party is a close friend of one of the combatants. Thus, we see that witnesses can be biased, if not outright deceptive.

This volume will cover the subjects of interviews and interrogations as thoroughly as possible. We'll look at the interpersonal techniques, the problems of detecting deception, and even survey the illegal methods, such as torture. This last is necessary, not to encourage the use of torture, but to make the reader aware that such things still happen. Some interrogators, furthermore, feel that they're justified in using torture, or at least illegal methods of coercion.

Throughout, this will be a practical guide for the interrogator, not an academic study. There is some history involved, to give the reader a perspective regarding how we got where we are today and to allow him to understand the mistakes of the past. Knowing history is also important to avoid re-inventing the wheel.

While some theory is inevitable, all theory presented in this book is aimed at furthering an understanding of the human personality with regard to interrogation. A certain amount of theory is important to avoid getting the reader bogged down in the byways and false trails of human personality.

Finally, this book will take a look at the future of interrogation, because further developments and refinements of techniques are inevitable. We'll examine present techniques and what they portend, even venturing into areas that right now are only science fiction. This is useful because, as almost everyone living in the Twentieth Century knows, today's science fiction is often tomorrow's fact.

THE HISTORY OF INTERROGATION

It's important to note at the outset that the history of interrogation is not the same as the history of torture. Physical torture, although effective, is crude. It's also counter-productive in many instances.

Scientific interrogation is truly a Twentieth-Century phenomenon. It's an adjunct to crime detection, and an allied technique. Interviewing is useful for examining witnesses and for pre-employment screening. Systematic criminal investigation did not exist before the Twentieth Century, although the groundwork came to be established in the prior century. Before then, interrogation was mainly an adjunct to religious practice. The Roman Catholic sacrament of "Confession" has the subject telling a priest of his sins and receiving forgiveness ("absolution") for them. This is a voluntary act, and not truly an interrogation. Although the priest may prompt the subject, he's not restrained or arrested in any way, and there's no coercion except the remote one of fear of dying with sins on the soul.

In ancient times, interrogations, such as they were, usually involved questions of faith. There were some criminal matters, and they were dealt with by a mix of ways, mostly involving eyewitness testimony. One widespread belief was that those who lied suffered dryness of the mouth. Ancient Hindus had a way of detecting and demonstrating this. The person making a statement had to chew rice and then spit it out upon a leaf. The presumption was that a liar would not be able to spit it out because his saliva would have dried up. During the Inquisition, a priest under examination would have his veracity tested by having to chew a piece of barley bread and some cheese. The dogma was that God would stop the throat of the liar.[1]

The original ends of interrogation were to obtain the truth and to obtain confessions. Confessions were extremely important in criminal trials, such as they were, and at the time, there was little thought given to the prospect that a confession obtained by duress might be invalid. Over the centuries, there arose a little more sophistication, and a recognition that interrogation really had two purposes, to obtain confessions and to obtain information.

In ancient Greece and Rome, torture was legitimate, and some of those we consider among the founders of Western culture, such as Demosthenes and Aristotle, endorsed it.[2] It is surprising, at first sight, that educated ancients, such as magistrates and high church officials, would not at times question whether torture was legitimate, and wonder if it was not possible to coerce an innocent person to confess with the application of enough pain. There was, however, what we today would call faith in the "system." It produced results, and it behooved even the insiders not to look too closely, not to "rock the boat." The torturers believed what they wanted to believe, that the people on whom they worked were, in fact, guilty and deserving of the most severe measures. Any refusal to confess simply meant that the subject was being stubborn, and was not an indication of innocence.

7

The methods change, but the mentality does not. We find the same sort of self-justifying thinking among polygraph examiners today, who turn a blind eye to the gaps and shortcomings of their craft and pretend near-infallibility.

In America, the Salem witch trials left behind accounts of alleged witches burned at the stake, although most of the alleged witches were actually hung. Another method used, but for criminal offenders, was the "ducking stool," loosely adapted from European practice. In this method, the subject was tied to a stool at the end of a long lever, and ducked into a pond or tank for longer and longer periods. The theory was that a criminal would be forced to confess by this treatment. Anyone who died was categorically proven to have had a pure heart.

In the United States, brutality in interrogations never disappeared. It diminished somewhat, and became very well hidden from view. The Nineteenth Century was the heyday of American police power. Rough-and-ready methods were not only permissible, but laudable. This was true of the entire spectrum of police work, where direct, goal-oriented methods were the rule. This is what led to the formation of the New York City Police Department's "Strong-arm Squad" in the middle of the Nineteenth Century. At the time, the Midtown area had a problem with muggers. The members of the Strong-arm Squad dealt with this simply and directly: upon sight of a known mugger, they beat him unconscious. "Curbstone Justice" was not only acceptable, but praised. This carried over into criminal interrogation. The Western and Southern sheriffs developed their reputations for "hand talk," a sobriquet for coercion-induced confession.

The process was gradually refined by its practitioners, who learned to distinguish between various types of leads obtainable during interrogations, and by colliding with the judicial system, which disapproved of forceful interrogation. Gradually, the "third degree" took form.

The third degree is largely undocumented, and knowledge of it exists in the realm of "street wisdom." One basic principle was to develop means of causing pain without leaving marks, because charges of police brutality were beginning to surface. An adjunct to this was to develop ways of covering up the violence that did occur. This was when police officers developed the excuses that the suspects had "bumped into a door," "fallen down a flight of stairs," or simply "resisted arrest" to explain the sometimes ghastly contusions and fractures that occurred.

The standard technique for handling a suspect during that era was to book him at the front desk, and then take him "upstairs" or "downstairs" to the detective squad room, or to the interrogation room, if there was one. The main point was to get him out of sight of the public. There would be a cursory attempt to persuade the subject to talk voluntarily. When this failed, the beating would begin. Some of the techniques for beating without causing fractures or contusions were:

1. Beating with a wet towel.

2. Using a soft blackjack.

3. Careful selection of areas to strike in order not to show marks. One favorite area was the kidneys.

4. Suffocation with a wet towel.

5. Dunking the subject's head into the toilet.

6. Arm-twisting.

7. Holding a towel soaked in ammonia over the subject's face.

These are the old-line American methods, and in one form or another they've been practiced all over the country. With the Twentieth Century, the techniques have changed somewhat. The stun gun has replaced the blackjack. The incidence of physical torture has diminished, partly because suspects now get to see family and attorneys shortly after arrest, instead of being incommunicado for days. Any wounds inflicted don't have time to heal, therefore.

During the early part of this century, there was some dabbling in psychological and chemical methods of inducing confessions. These were generally dead ends. "Truth serum" remained a legend, a tool of the mystery story writers, as suspects found it as easy to lie under drugs as they did normally. Hypnosis did not work on unwilling subjects. The "lie detector," the polygraph, received a lot of hype, but fell far short of its promise. The American fascination with gadgets had ample opportunities for fulfillment in the field of interrogation aids.

There's been a refinement of interrogation methods, with a growing realization that psychological methods can be very effective indeed. At first, these methods spread only by word-of-mouth, as the folklore and tradecraft of police work. Now the teaching of interrogation is systematized. Police officers study psychology, to blend it in with their on-the-job training, to carry out more efficient interrogations.

In other countries, the study of interrogation tools and techniques has been more systematized than in

America. The application of Pavlovian principles to the art has resulted in enhanced results. At the same time, certain legends have arisen, and these dominate the popular picture today. There are delusions that Iron Curtain interrogators have almost superhuman powers, and that nobody can resist.

Sources

1. *A Tremor in the Blood*, David Thoreson Lykken, New York, McGraw-Hill, 1981, p. 26.

2. *The Mugging*, Morton Hunt, New York, Signet Books, 1972, p. 104.

INTERROGATION IN THE MEDIA

The media treat interrogation in the same manner as they treat other aspects of police work: they distort. This is somewhat true in news reporting, where the unusual and sensational case receives emphasis while the commonplace rarely gets a mention. Thus, we read about a brutal police officer nearly killing a suspect in an effort to obtain a confession, but we never see the many routine interviews and interrogations involving neither fear nor violence.

News reporting tends to be selective, playing for maximum shock impact. After all, they're in business to sell papers. This is why the straight news media sensationalize the reporting.

The straight news results in distortion, but fictionalizing a subject is virtually a license to kill. A fiction writer, whether a novelist or screen writer, has only his imagination to limit him. This is why fictional detectives are so colorful and super-capable, and why TV and motion picture interrogations are a breed apart.

One popular image in Hollywood films of the war years has the Gestapo man threatening, "Ve haff vays of making you talk!" At the time, this was part entertainment, part war propaganda, and few questioned it. Film Gestapo men strutted through their scenes, warning their captives that "I can haff you shot!" if there was no cooperation forthcoming. Other threatening statements made famous by the Hollywood Gestapo were:

"If you do not cooperate, ve cannot be responsible for the safety of your family."

"You haff relatives in Chermany?"

Since the start of film-making, American police officers have fared no better. The dingy police station with its basement interrogation room is another stereotype. Of course, the stereotype was based originally on a grain of truth, and fifty years ago many police stations did have a dingy interrogation room in the basement, far enough from the street so that the suspect's cries of pain would be unheard outside. The subject is seated in a chair facing bright floodlights. The detective sits behind a desk, invisible to the subject. Several other policemen lounge about the room, sleeves rolled up, exuding an overtly menacing attitude. The questions are harsh and rapid: "You were there, weren't you? You did it, didn't you? Talk! Confess! We know all about it!"

The threat of violence as penalty for non-cooperation is always there, and sometimes breaks out into the open. Occasional police movies show suspects being beaten to force confessions.

A classic interrogation in American cinema appeared in the motion picture *Brute Force*, with Burt Lancaster, Hume Cronyn, and Sam Levine. This was a prison movie to top all previous ones. Burt Lancaster, the leader of a group of aspiring escapees, was about to be frustrated by the suspicions of the guard captain, Hume Cronyn. Cronyn, determined to get to the bottom of it all, brought Sam Levine to his office, where he set the scene for an outstandingly brutal interrogation. He handcuffed Levine to a table

13

and produced a blackjack. Walking over to the record player, he put on a record of Wagner, and turned the volume up. The music created the proper Wagnerian atmosphere for the interrogation and muffled Levine's cries of pain as Cronyn beat Levine's kidneys into pulp.

The films from the early era of Hollywood violence didn't lack intent, and were limited only by a very restrictive film production code. Violence was commonplace, but not very explicit. It was permissible to show shootings and beatings, but little blood and gore. Sam Levine, for example, was beaten in the kidneys where it wouldn't show, not in the face where the camera would pick up the broken bones and torn flesh created by a skillful make-up artist.

Recent films graphically depict violence, showing blood by the bucketful, but are also more restrained regarding interrogation violence. There's less violence for its own sake, a surprising aspect of any Hollywood operation. This is a reflection of an increasing trend towards realism. The net result, however, is that there's more violence and more explicit violence, because the film-makers tend to choose the more sensational and violent real-life events. The struggle between the Gaullists and the O.A.S. during the French Algerian War was very violent and brutal, and furnished much raw material for a number of films.

The film *The Day of the Jackal*, for example, shows an interrogation of an O.A.S. agent by French security service officers. The subject is strapped to a chair with electric wires attached to his body. In the novel, one is attached to his penis, and the other to his nipple. The film version isn't quite as explicit. One of the interrogators turns a rheostat periodically to punctuate his questions. The subject dies under this extremely painful treatment, but he "talks" enough to give the investigators a lead.

The foreign film producer can be as explicit as American ones, and sometimes more so. The Costa-Gavras film *State of Siege,* shows a secret police training session in explicit and painful detail.[1] A police captain from Uruguay, who has attended a police academy for foreign police officers run by the American "Agency for International Development" returns to his native land to instruct others. He brings with him a new interrogation device with which he's been supplied while at school. This is an electric shock machine, with leads, alligator clips, and electrodes for inflicting pain by electricity. In a demonstration before a class composed of other police officers, he uses the device on a male subject strapped naked in a chair. The film shows him touching an electrode to the victim's penis, and the victim's body convulsing.

A BBC television production *The Man From Moscow,* deals with the espionage careers of Greville Wynne, an English spy-businessman, and a Soviet traitor, Colonel Oleg Penkovsky. Both of these had showcase trials after their arrests, and the KGB did not present bloody hulks to the world press. The interrogation scenes are more restrained, in keeping with the real-life events.

An American TV production of the U-2 downing and its aftermath shows the American CIA pilot, Francis Gary Powers, being interrogated by a Soviet official who depends on calm persuasion instead of torture to bring Powers around. Powers' Soviet lawyer explains to him that, although his confession won't be necessary for a conviction, an expression of remorse would probably persuade the court to impose a lighter sentence. Powers, facing the prospect of spending the rest of his life in a Soviet

15

prison, conforms, and avoids having the tribunal "throw the book" at him.

No such civilized restraint mars the performances of the actors playing the parts of North Vietnamese POW camp officials in the recent round of Sylvester Stallone and Chuck Norris films. These productions both show and suggest gratuitous violence and degradation inflicted on American POWs in North Vietnamese hands.

The recent film *Red Dawn*, shows very moderate interrogation. The only scene showing an actual interrogation has the Communist colonel and his aide questioning the town mayor. The only severity inflicted on him in that scene is that he doesn't get to sit down. There is, however, a prison camp outside of town, presumably where dissident Americans are brought for some form of "re-education." The prisoners show signs of having been beaten, although it's not clear from the film whether this happened during arrest or "re-education." Eventually, some of the prisoners are shot in reprisal for American guerrilla raids.

We can see from this short discussion that the media treatment of interrogation is spotty. Some portrayals are accurate down to small details, while others are mostly imagination compounded by bad acting.

Sources

1. *Secret Police,* Thomas Plate and Andrea Darvi, Garden City, New York, Doubleday & Company, 1981, pp. 131-132. The information in these pages is remarkably congruent with the scenes in the Costa-Gavras film. Training methods for interrogators can be quite rigorous, even for the officers involved. The

subjects, of course, receive very little consideration, and have the status of experimental animals.

THE BASICS

All of the points regarding the interview or interrogation reflect back to the major theme: control. The interviewer must immediately establish control and seek to enhance his control as the interview or interrogation progresses. The amount of control possible will depend greatly on the situation. A witness can't be treated like an arrestee. Interviewers also vary greatly in the "presence" they demonstrate.

Whether the session is an interview or an interrogation, or whether the subject is a witness or suspect, there are certain very basic points to cover. There are also basic decisions to make which will have a far-reaching effect. The interviewer must do his homework, as prosaic and unglamorous as it might seem. The apparently trivial details can often make or break a case.

The first concern is the subject. Is communicating a problem? Can the subject speak English enough to be understood? If there's a problem with hearing or language, the interviewer must take steps to cope before starting the session. An interpreter can help, or the subject and interviewer can communicate in writing, if there's a hearing problem.

Foreigners sometimes feign lack of understanding of English to obstruct an interrogation. One way to test this is to hold a conversation regarding the subject in his presence. Making statements that are threatening to his well-being, such as announcing his impending arrest, may cause a display of emotion, if he understands.

An American interrogator who is fluent in a foreign language sometimes has an edge. A military policeman on patrol at a military base chased down a traffic offender who turned out to be a French-Canadian who pretended not to understand English. He chattered rapidly at the M.P.'s partner, who didn't understand French. He sprinkled his talk with insults such as "gros con," which the first M.P., having been born and raised in Belgium, understood well. After several minutes, the M.P. announced in French that the comedy was at an end, and that there would be appropriate citations issued.

There are at least two schools of thought regarding dress and demeanor. One is that the officer should be well-dressed, which usually means suit, white shirt, and tie, in order to look "professional." This dates from the days when being well-dressed was vaguely intimidating to those who were not. Today, people are more sophisticated, and even ghetto residents are "street-smart" despite lack of formal education.

The other viewpoint is that dress isn't very important, that substance is more important than form. An interrogator who knows his job will be more effective than a marginally competent dandy.

There are also two viewpoints regarding the atmosphere to establish for the session. One choice is an atmosphere of fear and menace. The other is the friendly and sympathetic ambiance. The choice depends a lot on the interviewer's personality and sophistication. Some police and private security officers are simply "badge-heavy," and always come across that way, even in routine public contacts. Others have a gift of dealing effectively with people, and don't need to rely on intimidation.

For psychological reasons which we'll cover later, the relaxed, friendly setting seems to work best most of the time. It's also the more logical, because it's always possible to take off the velvet glove to reveal the iron fist.

It's important to interview witnesses as soon as possible after the event, when memories are fresh. This is so important that it's worth compromising on other considerations. The locale may be noisy and distracting, but vividness of memory is fleeting, and the investigator must catch it when the moment comes.

Part of doing your homework is to have a list of topics to cover during the session. This can be a standard checklist or a few notes jotted down while investigating the case. This is far better than trying to "wing it."[1]

Many types of investigation are so routine that the investigator soon learns the points to cover by rote. This saves time in that he doesn't have to take notes for each case.

Another way is to memorize the journalist's checklist, the "7 Ws" — WHAT, WHEN, WHERE, WHY, HOW, WHO, and WHICH. We call this the "7 Ws" even though the fifth question doesn't start, but ends with a "W." The answers to these seven questions build the framework upon which the interrogator can work.

The interviewer should let the witness tell his story in his own way and in his own words first, preferably without interruption. This narrative form elicits the main points, and questions can fill in the details later.[2]

It's best to avoid leading questions during the interview. The investigator is trying to elicit what the witness knows, not influence his perception of the events. A leading question is one that suggests the answer, such as "Did you see the gun?" It's better to ask if he saw the suspect holding anything in his hands.

It may be necessary to prompt the witness. This is not the same as leading him. Prompting means encouraging him to continue with his account, pushing him along without steering him. Some examples of prompting are:

"What did you do then?"

"Why did you do that?"

"What else did you see at that moment?"

"Did you hear anything else right then?"

"Was anyone else there at the time?"

It often helps to nod "yes" at the witness while he's speaking, as acknowledgement of his statements and as encouragement to continue.

Take notes or not? In many instances, this is unimportant or the decision is out of the interviewer's hands. Routine matters, such as field interrogations, traffic accident investigations, and taking burglary or lost children reports, require filling in the forms. People are accustomed to this, and usually don't object to having their answers taken down for use in evidence. This is especially true in routine and commonplace investigations.

When interrogating a major case suspect, it may be advisable or at least permissible. If the suspect's a career criminal, there's no need for the interrogator to be overly concerned regarding whether the suspect's sensitivities will be offended by note-taking. A suspect who isn't a hardened criminal type needs more careful handling. Note-taking can seem threatening.

A frightened suspect may have his anxiety increased to the breaking point by the sight of a notebook. This is why a concealed tape recorder, permitted in almost all jurisdictions, is vital.

A major point is the locale of the interview. It should be in a quiet place with no distractions, but in the field this isn't always possible. Traffic investigations usually take place in a snarl of traffic, and the noise and sights are potentially distracting. However, most Americans manage to cope with this, concentrating on getting through rush-hour traffic despite the sensory overload.

Many other instances allow finding a quiet room for an interview. The witness's home or office is usually adequate, and often there's simply no choice. A witness is not a suspect, and an officer can't force a witness to accompany him to the police station.

When trying to construct a framework of the events, it's best to interview the witness most directly involved first. This gives the broadest picture, and the investigator can fill in the details later when interviewing others less directly involved. In an armed robbery, for example, the best witnesses are usually the people robbed, if they survived the experience, or those indoors if the crime took place in a building. They're the ones who probably had the longest look at the suspect or suspects, and who can furnish the most complete descriptions. Witnesses outside the building may have heard shots, or know the odd detail such as the plate number of the getaway car.

Even here compromises are often necessary. Getting the plate number can be the most important detail immediately needed to aid apprehension of the suspects. Usually, the first officer on the scene has taken care of this detail, and by the time the criminal investigator arrives the suspects' descriptions and other information are already on the air.

Taking statements from more than one witness enables cross-checking the important details. Any experienced investigator knows that witnesses are very fallible, and often don't remember events accurately. Witnesses will disagree on a suspect's height and weight, and even the color of his clothing. Coordinating and comparing the different accounts helps to reconcile discrepancies.

It also helps to cross-check the intangibles. Witnesses can be biased. This is an ever-present possibility where the witnesses know the suspects. In a domestic quarrel, for example, accounts from other householders and neighbors may be biased. Much depends on the relationship between the witness and the suspect, or the witness and the victim. Asking one witness how another got along with the participants gives another perspective, and helps to spot sources of bias.

Bias need not be deliberate lying. It can be merely a subtle shading or slanting of the facts, shown by selective reporting, connotations and comments to the side, and even intangibles such as facial expressions. The interviewer must be careful to perceive the witness's responses on several different levels, and to be watchful for evidence of bias.

It's necessary to be very careful in eliciting personal descriptions, because this process can be flawed in several ways. The fallibility of witnesses is well-known, and if the case comes to trial, the defense attorney will seek to exploit this to damage the witnesses' credibility. Attorneys also engage in other tactics permitted by our system of law. Any competent defense attorney will caution his client to change his appearance, and the change can be quite dramatic. A biker type looks quite different with a shave, haircut, and a business suit. A sleazy burglar or robber can look very respectable with normal cleaning-up and a change of clothing.

This is what makes photographing an arrestee immediately important. It's normal procedure to take "mug shots," but full length photographs are also necessary, because they show clothing and stance. Videotaping the subject is even better, because it adds the dimensions of movement and sound to the record.

In conducting a "line-up," the witness should get a look at the suspects before they have a chance to clean up and start changing their appearances.

Handling inadequate answers is a major problem for the interviewer. The witness may be purposefully evasive, or just may not know. It's best to use a light touch, such as re-phrasing the question. Returning to the topic later and from another direction can also prompt the witness's memory. If this doesn't work, the interviewer may try to discuss the reasons for the lapse of memory with the witness. Sometimes a witness will have hidden reasons for not being forthcoming. These reasons may be hidden only in that the witness doesn't bring them out during the interview, but they may be obvious to the interviewer.

A mother being asked about her son, a crime suspect, may be protective, and reluctant to disclose anything that will be damaging. This is a situation that the interviewer should approach with caution. Pointing out to the mother that evasions won't help her son is one way to do it. Mentioning that her credibility as a witness depends on her truthfulness is another tactic.

It's critically important not to be officious or "badge-heavy." The investigator must always keep in mind that he may need the witness's testimony in court. In this regard, it's important not to create excessive emotional tension when questioning witnesses. Avoid negative words such as "discrepancies," and never use the word "lie." Instead, refer to them as "points," which suggests minor matters that need to be "cleared up," or "clarified." This keeps the witness on your side, or at least neutral.

More subtle and elusive is the witness's confabulation. This happens when a witness doesn't remember details, but is reluctant to admit ignorance or lack of perception. Witnesses often make up details in order not to appear uninformed. It's hard to estimate how much this accounts for the discrepancies investigators find between accounts by different witnesses, but it points up the critical importance of cross-checking testimony.

Mastering the basics is vital for the interviewer. These serve as building-blocks for more involved and sophisticated techniques.

Sources

1. *The Gentle Art of Interviewing and Interrogation,* Robert F. Royal and Steven R. Schutt, Englewood Cliffs, New Jersey, Prentice-Hall, 1976, p. 54.

2. *Ibid.,* p. 99.

THE PSYCHOLOGY
OF INTERROGATION

We can better understand interrogation and how it works if we take a quick look at human psychology. This can be confusing, though, because we're dealing with intangibles, and there have been many "schools" of psychology. The beginning of the modern era began with Freud in the late Nineteenth Century. This quickly degenerated into a series of cat-fights with his "pupils," who broke off to found "schools" of their own. Jung, Adler, and others sought the gold at the end of the rainbow and also instant fame by starting their own clinics of psychoanalysis. These were from the start playthings of the rich. Unfortunately, this had more serious consequences than merely providing an expensive pastime for those who were perturbed and could afford the fees for psychoanalytic sessions. Psychoanalysis side-tracked Western psychology for many decades.

In many ways, psychoanalytic psychology is like religion. It deals with intangibles whose existence nobody can prove. There are competing factions, each with its own terminology. There's a lot of mutual jealousy, and accusations have passed between competing sects.

We're left with a number of psychoanalytic explanations for interrogation and brainwashing, and we have to dispose of these quickly before getting to the scientifically verifiable material. Let's therefore skip lightly over the main points, giving them the quick and dirty treatment they deserve.

The relationship between the interrogator and his subject becomes like that between the psychoanalyst and his patient, and "transference" quickly occurs. "Transference" means that the subject "transfers" the attitudes and emotions he had for his father onto the interrogator. The interrogator therefore appears as a "father figure," sternly bringing forth and exploiting the sense of "guilt" already in his subject. This means that, even if the subject is innocent of the accusation, his feelings of guilt will find expression, and he will therefore confess to what the interrogator directs.[1]

This is basically the psychoanalytic view of interrogation and the allied arts. It hasn't found much acceptance among the people doing the actual interrogations. The textbooks written by the experienced practitioners almost totally ignore psychoanalytic theory, instead concentrating on the nuts-and-bolts techniques. They do recognize, however, the effects of fatigue and the altered mental states fatigue brings. These are very important, and in our examination of the structure of the human nervous system, we'll see why.

SENSORY DEPRIVATION

This is a catch-phrase that has seen some use in discussions of prisoner interrogation and brainwashing. If the detainee has been confined to a small, dark cell, some say that he's been subjected to "sensory deprivation." This simply isn't true.

Sensory deprivation is an experimental technique

that was first tried about two decades ago. It consists of placing the subject in a tank of water heated to skin temperature and blocking out all light and sound. The subject hears and sees nothing, and floating in water deprives him of the feel of gravity. This can produce startling mental effects. Hallucinations are common.

True sensory deprivation requires special equipment, and sophisticated monitoring devices. Its usefulness in interrogation is open to doubt.

PAVLOV

Ivan Pavlov was a Russian psychologist and physiologist who did his most important work around the turn of the century, before the Communist government acceded to power. He won the Nobel Prize in 1904 for his work on the physiology of digestion, for example. For decades, his work was almost ignored on this side of the ocean, because the psychoanalytic theories, with their sexual connotations, were more titillating. Pavlov's work, however, was supported by rigorous experimentation, and has stood the test of time. A side-light on Pavlov is that he was not a fan of the Communist regime. The government tolerated him because of the unquestionable value of his work.

One side-effect of this ignorance of Pavlovian psychology was that an exaggerated fear of diabolical Soviet methods of interrogation arose in the West. Without the nature of Pavlov's work being widely known or understood, it was easy for slick magazine writers to present horrific pictures of irresistable methods of interrogation that would reduce any subject to putty. This also offered a convenient "cop-out" to those who had vested interests. When a

29

Western government found that one of its spies had been caught by the Soviets and put on trial, it was easy to deny the accusations, claiming that the defendent had been "brainwashed."

THE NERVOUS SYSTEM UNDER STRESS

At the outset, let's state clearly what many don't even consider, that human and animal nervous systems are remarkably similar. Humans tend to want to believe that they're incomparably superior to the lower orders of life, and attribute to themselves characteristics that seem imaginary, such as the "soul." We don't need to discuss religious concepts, however, to understand that humans and animals function in similar ways with other physical systems. All ingest and eliminate both solid and liquid matter. All have blood, and a biological pump, the heart, to circulate it. All have lungs and kidneys to replenish and clean the blood. None of this is controversial, and therefore it should not be surprising that the nervous systems of men and animals have many features in common.

It's also important to note that our systems function in essentially mechanical ways, beyond our control. This concept may seem revolting to those who argue for "freedom of the will," "human dignity," and other philosophical concepts. It's easy to understand, if we take the analogy of motor vehicles. All have motors, transmissions, fuel tanks, wheels, etc., whether they're Mercedes sedans or garbage trucks.

We can sum up Pavlov's psychological findings as follows:

There are basically four types of "temperaments" found in both men and dogs, upon which he experimented. These are "strong excitatory," "lively," "calm," and "weak inhibitory." These determine the basic personality type, and seem to be hereditary.

The "strong excitatory" type reacts strongly to stress, showing excitement and anger. This type can become wild and uncontrollable. The "lively" type reacts more rationally, although forcefully, to stress.

The other two types don't present such strong responses to stress. The "calm" type takes things in stride, and doesn't become very excited, while the "weak inhibitory" type tends to become paralyzed with fear. [2]

Pavlov conducted stress experiments in his work on the "conditioned reflex." This is setting up an association between a stimulus and a desired response. In practical terms, Pavlov found that his dogs salivated when presented with food. If he rang a bell each time he fed the dogs, after a while the dogs would learn to salivate at the sound of the bell.

Some of his experiments involved administering painful electric shocks to the dogs. He found that he could, by setting up conflicts, provoke neurosis in his dogs. He would, for example, apply a strong and painful electric shock at every feeding. The dog would simultaneously be hungry and fear the shock. This is what is called an "approach-avoidance conflict" and humans encounter counterparts in their daily lives.

Pavlov found that with enough stress, his dogs would "break down." They would have brain inhibition so that they became inactive. This happened first with the "strong excitatory" and "weak inhibitory" types. This was called "transmarginal inhibition."

Pavlov experimented with four types of stress. One was increasing the voltage until it became too much for the dogs to bear. Another was increasing the time lag between the sound of the bell and the food delivery. Anticipation took its toll.

The third way is very relevant to interrogation: providing confusing signals. Pavlov would sound the bell, then follow it with a shock instead of food. The fourth type of stress Pavlov used was debilitation, caused by fatigue, fever, or withholding nourishment. This, too, is a favorite forced interrogation tactic.

With stress that varied according to the individual dog's temperament, "transmarginal inhibition" occurred, as noted before. This had three stages of severity. The first was what Pavlov called the "equivalent" phase, in which all stimuli produced about the same reaction. We see this in severly fatigued people who take on an apathetic attitude. The expression "too tired to care" expresses it perfectly.

The next phase is the "paradoxical" one, in which there's a stronger reaction to weak stimuli than to strong ones. Again, we see this in people under stress, who "over-react." A small incident may set off a temper tantrum, for example.

The third stage is called the "ultraparadoxical" phase, and brings about a reversal of behavior. The type of behavior we would call "ultraparadoxical" in humans would be a change in beliefs or acceptance, such as a suspect accepting the police officer as a friend, admitting guilt, and eagerly signing a confession. This sudden shift from positive to negative or vice versa seems hard to understand, but we have enough real-life examples of people's reactions to stress to leave no doubt.

In the everyday world, we've seen sudden and seemingly inexplicable changes in behavior after a sudden and tragic incident. A teetotaler may, after the death of his wife, take to heavy drinking. The other side of the coin is that a drunk may, after a similar shock, suddenly abandon alcohol altogether. The one factor which disguises this sort of behavior is that people tend to rationalize, or explain away, their behavior rather than admit that they don't know why they're doing it.

Another of Pavlov's findings was accidental and came about when some of his experimental dogs were almost drowned. The animals were severely frightened, and after they became calm once more, Pavlov found that some of them had lost their conditioned reflexes. This happened to the ones which had shown transmarginal inhibition.[3] These were the "strong excitatory" and "weak inhibitory" types. The other two tended to resist stress better.

The experiences of both World Wars, with their mass psychiatric casualties, showed that men behaved in the same way as dogs. There were instances of men who had been decorated for bravery breaking down and becoming ineffective.[4] These developments provoked questions about the meaning of words such as "courage" and "cowardice." One of the results of the deepening understanding of the effects of stress on the human nervous system was the replacement of the term "shell-shock" by "battle fatigue." Both military psychiatrists and commanders realized that fighting men could stand only so much. In practical terms, a division would be severely impaired after more than about a hundred days of constant fighting. It was then necessary to replace it in the line and arrange for rest and rehabilitation.

There were systems devised to prolong the usefulness of fighting units in the line. It became standard practice to have two regiments of a division

33

at the front, with the third held in "reserve" a few miles to the rear.

INTERROGATION PSYCHOLOGY

Let's now look at interrogation practices and compare them with the four "stressors" Pavlov had listed.

Increasing the voltage was increasing the intensity of the stress. In everyday terms we could call this "putting on the pressure." Accusing a suspect and telling him of the severe consequences that are bound to follow is putting on mental pressure. Forcing him to stand naked and endure humiliation is another tried and true way that some police interrogators use.

Keeping a prisoner in isolation and spacing interrogation sessions far apart builds anticipation. So does promising early release and not allowing him to go free. Withholding favors of nourishment has a psychological effect.

Crossing the subject's signals is a widely-used technique. We see this in the "hot and cold" treatment, in which the interrogator is alternately friendly and hostile. Another variant is the "Mutt and Jeff" treatment, with one interrogator hostile and the other friendly.

Debilitation is the fourth technique, and the interrogator can weaken his prisoner in many ways, even killing him in the process. One way is simple fatigue. Ceaseless questioning will tire out even the strongest subject. Using relays of interrogators to keep the subject awake and talking is one way to do it. Another way is to have the guard keep the prisoner from sleeping. The interrogator goes home to get a night's sleep, but the prisoner has to march around the courtyard all night.

Excessive heat or cold are also fatiguing. A subject who is shivering won't be in the best shape after a few hours. Nor will one sweating profusely, as he risks heat stroke.

Withholding food and/or water is somewhat slower than fatigue, but the slowness of onset also brings more profound effects. A starving subject also fatigues more quickly.

It's significant that some of the tactics used by interrogators overlap between the four stressors. Putting the pressure on works to increase the intensity of the stress and also to provoke fatigue. The good guy/bad guy routine crosses the subject's signals and also puts pressure on him. It also produces emotional fatigue. Torture, of course, works on several levels. At the outset, it's severe pressure. It causes extreme emotional tension, and physical excitement. The adrenal glands secrete more than usual, the blood pressure and pulse rate rise, and respiration increases. These physical reactions quickly bring on fatigue.

With the Pavlovian classifications as a basis, we can easily understand how the effects of interrogation come about. The loss of identity some describe comes about through pressure and fatigue. Fatigue increases suggestibility, and the subject accepts the guilt that the interrogator passes off onto him. No matter how much the subject is convinced of his innocence initially, as the stress increases he approaches the breaking point. This is where the transmarginal inhibition sets in. Beyond this point, the subject shows bizarre behavior. He becomes apathetic to normal things. He starts to over-react. Finally, he breaks down completely and believes his guilt in the ultraparadoxical phase. Not only does he believe it, but he enthusiastically accepts it as he once accepted his innocence.

This is what accounts for the strange behavior of those who have been through this sort of interrogation. The Moscow trials showed the world that once-loyal party men were traitors. The documented cases in the West of innocent persons wrongfully convicted because of faulty interrogation present the other side of the coin. As we study interrogation tactics, we'll see how the Pavlovian principles pervade the field, and dominate the methods.

Sources

1. *Battle for the Mind*, William Sargant, Garden City, New York, 1957, p. 148.

2. *Ibid.*, p. 32.

3. *Ibid.*, p. 41.

4. *Ibid.*, pp. 47-60.

THE INTERVIEWER'S QUALITIES

Interviewers and interrogators need certain personal qualities to help them in their jobs. Few of these qualities are in any way inborn. All can be cultivated or improved. This is very much like considering the intangible trait, "leadership." There are some "natural-born leaders," of course, but it's also possible to learn the techniques. The military services have leadership schools, and universities teach leadership techniques as part of a business administration program. Long experience has led practitioners of the craft to analyze their techniques so that they may instruct others.

Let's examine the traits an interrogator should have, separating fact from fiction, and arrive at a good guide to how to develop the qualities needed.

1. The interrogator must, above all, be able to keep his emotions under control. This means refraining from the display of negative emotions and the ability to simulate emotions when appropriate. It includes the ability to act.

It's been stated that a successful interrogator has to be an actor, putting on a show for the subject. This is true, but it's an over-simplification. Most often, it's necessary to keep a cool manner under difficult circumstances.

The interrogator may loathe a suspect who's accused of a revolting crime. An officer with children may be utterly revolted by a sex criminal or child murderer. Regardless, he must maintain a neutral manner or risk blowing the interrogation.

It's also necessary to avoid showing frustration or impatience with a difficult subject. A friendly witness will be alienated if the interviewer is harsh with him. A suspect may try to provoke the interrogator into losing his temper, to get a hold on him. We'll return to this theme in discussing "street smarts."

2. The interrogator must be able to dissemble while appearing sincere. This is part of the acting ability required. It's often necessary to mislead a subject in subtle ways, and the interviewer must be able to play the role. Not only is it necessary to hide strong negative emotions, but it's necessary to show a friendly and sympathetic manner, especially when the subject's confessing. Simulating approval takes some acting ability, and is a deception of mood rather than a deception in fact.

Cultivating a "sincere" manner is the core of this talent. A direct gaze, looking deeply into the suspect's eyes, helps get across the impression of sincerity. Think of the folklore regarding the behavior of liars — the shifty eyes, the evasive speech — and consciously avoid these during an interrogation. Practice suppressing any mannerisms that a subject might interpret as "fidgety," and which might lead him to doubt your sincerity.

3. Learn to project sympathy and empathy. This is necessary with many subjects, and an interrogator who can convince his subject that he understands how he feels will get better results than one who projects a cold and unsympathetic manner.

A suspect who has murdered his wife, for example, may be very responsive to an interrogator who gets the point across that he understands how stressful marriage can be. Convincing the subject that you understand because you're married yourself, and in the same situation, can build a bond that's intangible but no less real, and prepare the way for cooperation.

Sometimes the communication need not be verbal. A sympathetic pat on the shoulder implies more than words, yet does not commit the interrogator to any course of action. A defense lawyer cannot accuse the interrogator of breaking a promise when the communication is non-verbal.

4. It's essential to be "street-smart." The subjects often are, and despite lack of formal education, they are quite alert and capable of defending themselves in verbal encounters. The career criminal is typically street-smart, with an ability to play upon other peoples' sympathies and to take advantage of any of their doubts or weaknesses.

The street-smart subject has developed an ability to quickly "size-up" the person he's facing, and to exploit the advantages in the situation. Interrogators quickly become accustomed to the extreme aggressiveness shown by suspects who try emotional blackmail.

This can happen on the simplest and lowest level. One street-smart subject, stopped by an officer for a traffic citation, accused the officer of bigotry and of citing him only because he was Hispanic.[1]

Suspects may try other ploys:

"Why are you picking on me? Can't you find the guy who really did it? Just because I have a record, you think I'm the one for everything that comes down around here."

This is an example of how a street-smart suspect can distort his rendering of the situation in an effort to put the interrogator on the defensive. He even tries to manipulate the officer by taking advantage of the fact that he has a criminal record.

On a lower level, the street-smart subject knows how to create distractions to cover his evasiveness. Persistent and repeated requests to go to the toilet, for example, are ways of getting away from the tension of the interrogation and buying time to think of answers to questions. Complaints of unfair treatment, while obviously spurious, can side-track the interview, especially if the interrogator loses control of his temper.

The street-smart subject will also be sensitive to the possibility of a "deal." Sometimes he'll ask for one. At other times he'll listen carefully to any stated or implied promise of a deal by the interrogator.

5. The interrogator should be intelligent, but not "brain-proud." Being intelligent doesn't mean an obligation to show it off at every opportunity. It's best to play it low-key, although not try to appear dull-witted. The TV character, Columbo, was a parody, although in the scripts he seemed to disarm his suspects adequately.

Intelligence goes well with the next quality, because the main advantage of high intelligence is the ability to keep quiet and think.

6. The interrogator should be very aware, and develop the ability to observe critically. A well-known quote from Sherlock Holmes is his admonition to Watson; "You see, but you do not observe." Many people go through their lives overlooking the obvious because of a dull mental attitude. They're not stupid, but don't use what mental capacity they have.

Experienced interviewers know that people will say the most amazing things at times. Paradoxical as it may seem, people have confessed to murder without any threat or coercion inflicted upon them. Sometimes it's possible to explain these happenings away by vague comments about "guilt feelings," but they're not entirely satisfactory because they don't really explain why the person should suddenly feel guilty.

In other instances, people admit very significant facts, seemingly without awareness that they're delivering damaging testimony. People do have mental lapses, and taking advantage of them when they come is an important part of an interviewer's job.

A more practical reason for the subject's giving away admissions freely is simply lack of coordination. Co-conspirators don't always have their "stories" straight before interrogations. There are discrepancies because they never agreed upon what to say to the police, and the interrogator can exploit these discrepancies to break the case wide open.

7. The interrogator must be thorough. This is necessary to pay proper attention to the many details that make up a case.

This doesn't require a fantastic memory. It only requires that the interrogator approach his job in a systematic way, keeping his evidence in an orderly manner. It's also not necessary to memorize everything. Written records serve well, as long as the investigator can lay his hands upon the parts he needs when he needs them.

Another way in which it pays to be thorough is to exploit cooperation from a suspect. A confession isn't enough, and an investigator who rejoices in his victory and rests upon his laurels may be disappointed in court. After a session with a lawyer, a suspect can repudiate a confession. This is easy to do because of the reputation of police for extorting confessions. An accusation of brutality or coercion is easy to make and sustain in order to have a confession ruled inadmissible.

Exploiting a confession means securing knowledge of corroborating evidence which can be useful in case the defendant repudiates his confession. It's also possible to develop other investigative leads that will permit conviction of confederates. A variety of information is accessible once the subject decides to cooperate.2

8. Patience is a virtue, especially in interrogation. The interrogator needs patience, not only to plow through the mass of details that make up his case, but to endure the verbal ploys that subjects use endlessly. An interrogator who loses his patience can also lose important details of a case. If he loses his patience during an interrogation, he can also lose his temper, and possibly lose his case.

The interrogator must have patience with people, not only the sleazy suspects, but the many ordinary people who turn up as witnesses. Witnesses, as we've seen, are fallible, and even make up details. Patience in reconciling conflicting testimonies is vital to putting together a coherent picture of the case. It also takes patience to deal with a witness who is confabulating, and to separate fact from fiction.

9. Stamina is important. It's necessary to have emotional stamina to sustain the intense adversary relationship with a suspect. The battle of wits can be emotionally exhausting, and the one with the most endurance has an edge in becoming the winner.

It's also necessary to have physical stamina.

Interrogation can take a long time and impose a physical toll upon the body. Being able to outlast the subject can be beneficial. Fatigue plays an important role in interrogation, and wearing the subject down can lead to a confession.

BREAKING DOWN THE MYTHS

Let's now examine what an interrogator doesn't need, or at least can do without. There have been some myths fostered by ill-informed people, and these myths, because of a superficial logic, have taken hold enough to be widely believed.

One myth is that the interrogator must be an older person, to play the role of "father-figure." [3] This is a good example of "pop-psych," and although it seems logical at first, has little or no basis in fact.

There are some very competent, and very experienced, interrogators in middle age. These are the ones usually cited to uphold this point. The indisputable fact is that these successful interrogators weren't born at age 40. They started interrogating subjects at the start of their careers and must have shown aptitude for it in order to continue and attain distinction.

The idea of a subject placing his trust in a "father figure" can hold water only if he admired and trusted his father. Many people, especially career criminals, show a pattern of behavior that we call "rebellion against authority." It's hard to see how this sort of person would react positively to a "father figure."

We can also argue that the subject's likely to confide in a peer-substitute, someone of his own age and sex. He may, or he may not, but we can find ample psychological theory to "prove" that he will.

Another myth is that of the cold, competent, calculating machine. The interrogator doesn't have to be a walking computer, with a "steel-trap" mind, who picks up on every discrepancy. This bizarre sort of figure seems threatening, anyway, and can be counter-productive.

Yet another is the physically brawny detective who uses physical methods to force confessions. While in some instances, there is torture used, anyone who looks like a "goon" will have a hard time of it. The intimidating effect on the suspect may be beneficial, but largely outweighed by the majority of instances where physical force is inappropriate. If ever there is an accusation of brutality, the interrogator who gives the impression of a "goon" is handicapped from the start.

Another myth pertains to ridicule. Supposedly ridicule is a devastating weapon and unsuitable for use in an interview or interrogation. This is only half-true. It's unwise and brutal to ridicule a witness who is trying to help. This is poor public relations and can only alienate the witness. It's another matter when a "street-smart" suspect is trying a ploy to upset the interrogation. Under these circumstances, trying to reason or argue with the suspect is a waste of time, and only side-tracks the interrogation. Ridicule is one way of short-circuiting the attempt, losing as little time as possible.

PERSONAL DEVELOPMENT

Good interrogators can be made, as well as born. Most of the skill is simple dedication and hard work, not intuitive brilliance. In this book, we'll examine the techniques and facets of interrogation from several different viewpoints, and lay out the different styles of interviewing and interrogation. Tactics and technique are at the heart of becoming a competent interrogator. Study and practice are the keys.

Sources

1. Witnessed by the author many years ago. Unfortunately, in this instance the officer fell for the ploy and wasted a quarter-hour arguing with the subject, risking the possibility of an escalation.

2. *Criminal Interrogation,* Arthur S. Aubry, Jr., and Rudolph R. Caputo, Springfield, Illinois, Charles C. Thomas, Publisher, 1980, pp. 24-25.

3. *The Gentle Art of Interviewing and Interrogation,* Robert F. Royal and Steven R. Schutt, Englewood Cliffs, New Jersey, Prentice-Hall, Inc., 1976, pp. 133-134.

A CLOSE LOOK AT LIES

Lies are important in a discussion of interrogation because they bear strongly on the central issue, obtaining accurate information. In many instances, people will lie, tell white lies, tell half-truths, and omit significant facts. The investigator's task is to elicit the information, however reluctant the subject may be. For this, it's necessary to understand the anatomy of the lie, and the forms it may take.

The first type of lie to consider is the purposeful misstatement. This is the outright and obvious lie, and requires no further discussion.

The next, but far from obvious, is the lie by concealment or omission. This is the purposeful withholding of information or material facts.

The third is the lie by indirection. This means giving an answer that is not an answer, one that's cleverly worded to give the wrong impression without stating an outright lie. Sometimes, this can take the form of answering a question with a question: "Do you think I'd really do a thing like that?" There are other verbal tricks used by skillful liars, such as telling the truth humorously, or in an exaggerated manner.

All of these are lies. They often work in casual conversation, even between long-time friends, but any professional interrogator who allows himself to be manipulated by some of these verbal ploys is inept. It's easy to cut some of the games short.

Anyone who answers a question with a question can be put in his place with the curt statement: "I'm asking the questions here." Other tricks can be dismissed with a simple "Better decide whether you want to play games, or give me straight answers." The police investigator, unlike the journalist, has the power of the criminal justice system behind him, and he can use it to enforce compliance.

In a lie, intent is everything, and the investigator must be aware of the subject's interests and needs in order to place his statements in proper perspective. It's obvious that someone accused of a crime is likely to want to deny it to escape punishment. Sometimes, the relationship isn't crystal clear. A person may admit guilt falsely to shield another. This is where familiarity with the facts of the case will be helpful in untangling motives. The investigator must always think on several levels. He must consider the need to obtain evidence, the subject's need to avoid implicating himself any more than he has to, and the roles of other parties in the case.

CATCHING LIES

People vary in their ability to detect liars. Some are very inept, and others, in laboratory situations, have been successful about 85% of the time.[1] These figures aren't very important, because they don't really relate to the outside world. A laboratory experiment in which one person tells lies while the other tries to discover them by studying his behavior isn't at all like a real-life police investigation. The investigator has many more cues than mere superficial behavior to guide him. The adversary, too, has much more at stake than in a laboratory test.

Similarly, people vary in the ability to tell lies convincingly. Some have no confidence in their ability to get away with a lie, convinced that they'll be found out. Others, made confident by years of practice in telling convincing lies, can pass off falsehood for truth very readily and well. [2]

Such people are not necessarily criminals or sociopaths. They're merely skillful liars. These tend to gravitate into life situations where they can exploit this skill to manipulate people. Some likely occupations are salesman, doctor, and psychologist.

LIES AND INTERROGATIONS

Case preparation is the important preliminary step to an interrogation. [3] This means knowing all of the available facts, and planning an approach to the subject. The investigator who's armed with the facts has an important advantage over the subject who doesn't know how much the police know.

There are several cues to a lie. One of the most important, and the most damning, is inconsistency with known facts. A suspect who claims that he drove his car from one place to another is in a bad way when the investigator points out that his car was in for repair on the day in question. Another is an internal contradiction. A subject who tells one version and later presents another, has a lot to explain away. This is an important reason for tape-recording interviews and interrogations. Playing the subject's voice back to him can be shattering if the previous version contradicts what he's trying to sell now. A recorded voice is beyond denial in such a situation.

In this respect, any experienced interrogator knows that a subject will often miss out on minor details. This is because people don't remember unimportant facts clearly. Experience with witnesses shows that many people don't notice important information, such as the clothing worn by a suspect. Often, to avoid appearing uncertain or saying they don't know, they will confabulate to fill in the blanks. The interrogator can use these discrepancies to put pressure on the subject, if he can't catch him in other mis-steps.

The suspect's manner can cue the interrogator to an attempt at deception. There are some verbal and physical signs that may indicate deception. The main point here is that there is no unmistakeable physical or emotional sign that the subject's telling a lie. The interrogator must form a judgment based on several ambiguous verbal and physical cues.

VERBAL INDICATORS

What we call "slips of the tongue" or "Freudian slips" can be clues to deception. A person sometimes spits out something involuntarily, and this often reveals an emotion rather than a fact. This is especially true during a "high-pressure" interrogation where the investigator snaps out questions as quickly as the subject produces answers. The subject can become confused, or involuntarily say "yes" when he means "no." This is why a hastily-uttered error isn't truly significant. People watch what they say very carefully, and the truth isn't likely to come pouring out in an involuntary confession.

The tone of voice, and the pitch and rhythm of the words, can change during deception. However, they also change during strong emotion. It's futile trying to draw conclusions from the tone of voice without knowing what the person's voice is like in normal times, when he's not under the stress of an investigation. Occasionally, a subject will lose control during an interrogation and, under the influence of strong emotion, will spit it all out. This is more likely to happen with the situational offender than the career criminal.

The situational offender is the person who normally walks the straight and narrow but, on one occasion, has committed a criminal act. It may have been theft to cover a crushing debt, or a killing after great provocation. Laden with guilt, as well as the fear of being caught, he "breaks down" and lets it all out. It's hard to imagine a professional criminal becoming so upset during an investigation.

Another verbal cue is the evasive answer. A person who during the interrogation has been giving crisp replies but suddenly becomes cagey and evasive when the topic shifts to a sensitive point, may be deceptive. It can also work the other way, as when a liar becomes very verbose and volunteers too much information. It's very important to have a "feel" for the subject's normal speech pattern, because some people typically give circumlocutory answers.[4]

BODY LANGUAGE

There are some physical signs that can reveal additional information that the subject won't verbalize. Some of this is what we call "body language," a set of gestures and postures that communicate an attitude or emotion rather than a fact.

In one spectacular laboratory experiment of a few years ago, a number of college students were filmed

50

as they attended interviews with a professor who purposefully was very critical of them. One of the students showed the finger gesture while in the interview. The student was unaware of this, and the professor could not recall seeing it. Only the film, which substantiated this behavior, was convincing.

This category of behavior is called an "emblem." It's a gesture with a definite meaning, which often varies from one culture to another.5 One is the "finger" gesture. Another "emblem" is the "ba fangool" gesture of the fist in the elbow. Yet another is the shrug, which often denotes ignorance or helplessness. While emblems are typically deliberate and purposeful gestures, they sometimes happen as "slips," and can betray an emotion. They also happen under the influence of strong emotion. A person who presents a "ba fan-gool" gesture is angry, and an observer won't need to depend on the gesture as a sign of anger. It'll probably be obvious from the tone of voice and facial expression, as well as the speech contents.

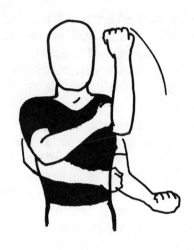

The usefulness of this in a criminal investigation is hard to see. An investigator wouldn't be too surprised if a hardened criminal flipped him a "bird," inadvertently or not. The gesture would certainly not be proof of guilt.

Another type of gesture is known as the "illustrator." There are two types of illustrators. One is a descriptive gesture, meant to help explain a concept. A person may make a chopping motion with his hand to describe a sudden event, or spread his hands apart, palms inward, to describe something huge. The other use for an illustrator is to emphasize a point. There are some cultural differences in the use of these illustrators.6

People who normally use illustrators may use them less under certain circumstances. Indecisiveness or lack of emotion can cause a decrease in the use of illustrators. Excitement can cause an increase. An attempt to fabricate a careful lie can also cause a decrease.

One combination that Paul Ekman identifies as a possible clue to deception is an increase in emblems and a decrease in illustrators.7 This is tentative, not conclusive. Let's keep in mind that laboratory work doesn't necessarily correspond to street conditions.

Yet another type of body movement is the "manipulator." This is a stroking, rubbing, or picking gesture, such as smoothing the mustache or hair, picking the nose, or scratching the skin. These are what most people consider signs of "nervousness," and they show that the subject is under stress.

Facial expressions are also alleged to be clues to deception. Unfortunately for the lie detector, this reasoning also breaks down. There are several reasons why facial expressions aren't reliable guides.

One is that individuals are different, both anatomically and in the way they react to situations. Even if we accept that there are certain expressions associated with certain emotions, they'll vary from one person to the next.

There are also cultural differences. In some cultures, it's normal to display emotions by vivid expressions. Members of other cultures act in a way that we can best describe as "deadpan." One manifestation of this is the widely-held view that Orientals are "inscrutable." This is the result of their acting very restrained in front of strangers, and most Westerners are strangers to them. In private, or with family and friends, they can be as emotional as others.

At the opposite extreme are those whom we regard as "excitable," such as the Italians. Typically, Italians use gestures more than many other groups, and in common with other Latins, their voices rise and fall in intonation more than is customary in other cultures. However, it would be a mistake to judge a stranger to be of Italian ancestry because of voice intonation or gesticulations. Likewise, there's much variation between individuals in the same group. The generalizations break down when we try to apply them to individual cases.

It's important not to make too much of these signs, either. The interrogator cannot know if the subject is showing more "nervousness" than usual unless he knows how much is "normal" for the subject. Another obvious fact to consider is that the signs of anxiety may be perfectly accurate, but subjects feel anxiety for a variety of reasons. It's quite normal to feel anxious when suspected of a crime. A victim feels injured and anxious, or even apprehensive that the perpetrator may return to do more harm. The emotional after-shock of being a crime victim isn't appreciated or understood enough by police officers.

A liar may not feel any guilt or anxiety. Anyone telling a "white lie" may well not feel guilty or anxious. Salesmen and con artists accept lies as tools of their trades. A career criminal, likewise, sees lying to the police as normal, and doesn't feel any guilt. There are many such people and situations.8 Taking all of these factors into account, we can understand why there's no unequivocal symptom of lying.

The myth, however, persists. Even today there's a belief that a liar can't look the other person in the eye. This is supposed to be the result of interference of nerve impulses in the brain.9 We can, if we wish, find an entire catalog of "Symptoms of Deception," based on the classical beliefs that have proven to be a mixture of half-truths and myths.10

One tactic that's open to the interrogator is to point out to the suspect that he's perspiring, and to cite this as evidence of guilt.11 There's a more likely alternative explanation which throws the whole matter into doubt. Perspiration is a symptom of emotional stress. A suspect, innocent or guilty, will be under stress when faced with an interrogator who refuses to believe him. The interrogator who seizes upon this and compounds the stress by an outright accusation of deception will be following a destructive spiral if he's wrong, and the suspect is indeed telling the truth. This is what Paul Ekman has called the "Othello Error," and there's reason to believe that it's very common.12

LYING: A LEARNED SKILL?

Lying is a skill, or set of skills. Both laboratory evidence and practical experience show that some people are better at it than others. This isn't surprising, because people in general differ in competence in many fields. With lying, however, it's hard to judge how much of it results from inborn talent and how much is learned. This is simply because not much work has been done on the subject.

There are schools and training courses for many other interpersonal skills, such as "leadership," "counseling," etc. There is no school for liars, and it's not likely that there will be one in the foreseeable future. There is, however, a written study of how to lie, which we'll cover in the chapter on surviving interrogation.

Sources

1. *Telling Lies,* Paul Ekman, New York, W.W. Norton Co., 1985, p. 87.

2. *Ibid.,* pp. 56-7.

3. *The Gentle Art of Interviewing and Interrogation,* Robert F. Royal and Steven R. Schutt, Englewood Cliffs, New Jersey, Prentice-Hall, 1976, pp.51-58. It's hard to exaggerate the importance of "doing your homework" in setting up for an interrogation. Careful spadework before asking the first question can save hours of verbal probing and fencing.

4. *Telling Lies,* p. 91.

5. *Ibid.,* pp. 99-103.

6. *Ibid.,* pp. 105-109.

7. *Ibid.,* p. 108.

8. *Ibid.,* pp. 67-72.

9. *Criminal Interrogation,* Arthur S. Aubry, Jr., and Rudolph R. Caputo, Springfield, Illinois, Charles C. Thomas, Publisher, 1980, p. 247.

10. *Ibid.,* pp. 244-255.

11. *Ibid.,* p. 248.

12. *Telling Lies,* p. 170.

THE INTERROGATION LOCALE

Although friendly witnesses can be interviewed in a variety of places, the place to interview a suspect must meet certain criteria. Because control is very important with regard to a suspect, the location must be physically secure. It's not necessary to interrogate in a cell, or a room with bars on the windows, but there must be very visible deterrents to escape.

The interrogator must understand fully the importance of the locale, and the reasons why police adhere to certain practices in setting up interrogations. Decades of experience have shown that isolation of the suspect is critically important in obtaining information, evidence, and confessions. One event that upset this procedure was the Miranda Decision.

The official objection of police officers to the Miranda Decision is that the petty and common criminal now has the same rights previously enjoyed only by the affluent or sophisticated criminals. This allegedly has cut down on the percentage of confessions obtained because nowadays suspects are advised explicitly that they don't have to talk.

This sounds logical, but it's an over-simplification. As we'll see, the Miranda Decision has had more far-reaching effects than making suspects aware of their rights. The right to consult an attorney immediately has broken up the pattern of emotional isolation that many interrogators feel is helpful in creating the right atmosphere. We'll examine this closely.

The locale of the interrogation is critically important. There are several practical psychological reasons for this:

1. Removing the subject to an unfamiliar locale starts the feeling of isolation and disorientation. The ability to uproot him from his home and neighborhood is also a tangible manifestation of the power that the police have over him. It establishes control, the basic pre-requisite to a successful interrogation.[1]

2. A basic rule is to keep the subject isolated, especially from friends and possible co-conspirators. This deprives him of emotional support and reassurance. Isolation interferes with group support and starts to nibble away at bonds of loyalty. It also prevents collusion between suspects, which might foil an interrogation. It may surprise some that this was a tactic used by the Communists in Korea, in the "brainwashing" of POWs. [2]

3. Isolation also means solitary confinement when not in the interrogation room. This tends to build apprehension without the prospect of "ventilation," talking it out with a friend or fellow-prisoner.

4. Isolation also allows the interrogator to control what the subject sees and hears. The interrogator can feed him what news he deems fit, and can slant the news to suit his purposes. Telling the subject that his fellow-conspirators have confessed, for example, can be devastating if it's possible to make the subject believe it.

Allowing contact with an attorney shortly after arrest precludes keeping the suspect isolated and alienated. In many instances, the suspect's allowed a phone call, which often is to a relative. This emotional sustenance helps the prisoner's resolve, and lets him know that someone out there cares for him, is aware of his plight, and is obtaining help. Contact with the outside world also helps the suspect to maintain an even keel. He's less vulnerable to mis-information from the police.

In the days before the Miranda Decision, police used to go to great lengths to keep their suspects isolated. In the Leopold-Loeb case, Chicago police kept moving the arrestees from one police station to another, because the suspects' wealthy families had hired lawyers to present writs of habeas corpus. These would have gotten the suspects an immediate hearing, and possible release, if the lawyers had been able to catch up with them.

With complete control of the suspect, the interrogator can increase his emotional tension and wear him down by isolation. This allows him to take breaks while relegating the suspect to his cell, alone, to think about his plight.

Even with the Miranda Decision, it's possible to isolate the suspect. Some suspects are so cocksure that they feel they don't need an attorney. In other instances, the attorney requested by the suspect isn't immediately available.

The interrogation room should be quiet, and preferably insulated from street and office noises. If there are windows, they should have blinds, shades, or drapes, to minimize visual distractions. While it's not necessary that the room be utterly drab, the decor should be simple, not garish. The furnishings should be simple: a desk, and enough chairs to accommodate several people. The room should be one specially set aside for interrogations, not a borrowed office. This is so that no objects of value, or distracting objects, are in the room. It would be undesirable to have a suspect rifling drawers if it's necessary to leave him alone in the room for a few minutes.

If there's a telephone on the desk, it should not be an incoming line because the ringing of the phone at a critical moment can break the mood. The telephone is useful for setting the scene. If it's connected to only one other phone, another officer can use it to place a fake "call" to the room, which the interrogator can exploit to mislead the subject.

The physical location isn't as important as what goes on during the interrogation. The interpersonal relationship between the subject and the interrogator is the main determinant. The key factor is "rapport," which we'll examine next.

Sources

1. *The Gentle Art of Interviewing and Interrogation,* Robert F. Royal and Steven R. Schutt, Englewood Cliffs, New Jersey, Prentice-Hall, 1976, p. 22.

2. *The Manipulated Mind,* Denise Winn, London, The Octagon Press, 1983, p. 9. This deals with the efforts of the captors to break up any affiliations between members of the group, in order to foster the feeling of isolation. Part of this was an abolition of leadership, so that the prisoners would not have any chain of command or authority figures. Page 36 describes how prisoners were also isolated from communication with home. This fostered the feeling of abandonment, and increased alienation.

RAPPORT

Establishing "rapport" with the subject is the objective at the opening of the session. The interrogator introduces himself if they've not yet met, and starts off with small talk. This serves two purposes. The first is that it helps to relax the subject, who may have been anticipating a more severe manner.

The second purpose isn't as obvious. Small talk, leading to rapport, conditions the subject to talking. The subject may have come into the room determined not to answer any questions and furthermore not to say a word. It's relatively easy to keep silent in front of an interrogator who immediately starts soliciting information about the crime or a confession. It's much more difficult to resist one who's non-threatening and who shows a friendly manner. Once the interrogator's got the subject talking about something, he'll tend to continue talking, and the longer the subject can be drawn out in this way, the harder it'll be for him to shut up when the interrogator veers the conversation into a channel dealing with the main topic.

Often, the subject will need careful handling. A situational offender, in contrast to the hardened criminal, is probably frightened and remorseful. A sympathetic manner can quickly calm him, overcome resistance, and get him talking. There's a definite difference between a sympathetic manner and being overly friendly, which is a mistake.

When dealing with the situational subject, it's possible to start encouraging emotional "clinging." The situational offender is likely to have committed a vehicular homicide or a sex crime. Even if he's killed someone in the heat of an argument, he's probably traumatized and emotionally vulnerable when inside a police station, wondering what will happen to him next.

The point behind starting with a neutral topic, and then moving to some innocuous questions, is to build "commitment."[1] Psychologists often have exotic terms for something commonly known by a simpler name. In this case, "commitment" is known colloquially as the "salami technique."

The idea is that it's difficult to ask a person to give you an entire salami at once. Asking for a single slice will more likely produce results. Asking for it slice by slice can often bring in the whole salami. In a rougher sense, this is what aggressors often do to gain their ends without a fight. They make small, but progressive encroachments. No single step provokes the victim to say, "No! This is the line where I stand and fight!" Thusly, an aggressor, whether an individual or a nation, can creep up on his victim and attain his ends "peacefully."

Likewise, the salami technique in an interrogation avoids mobilizing the subject's anxiety. He keeps telling himself that there's no harm in answering a few questions about his hobbies, or his family. Using this technique deprives the subject of a sharp and clearly definable point at which he can dig in his heels and resist.

During this introductory period, the interrogator starts building his persona, or image. It's important to appear strong, in the sense of being someone on whom the subject can lean if he wishes. Appearing strong does not mean cultivating a harsh, abrasive, or judgmental manner. Anyone who appears punitive will foreclose any chances of getting a subject to open up quickly.

Confidence and respect are the key words, but attaining these in the subject isn't easy. It's necessary to appear strong and firm without bullying or antagonizing. It's necessary to demonstrate an air of confidence and competence, but without going overboard to make the subject feel stupid.

One way to appear strong is never to seem indecisive. The interrogator who projects an aura of knowing exactly where he's going builds this sort of respect. To demonstrate strength and decisiveness, always give orders firmly. Upon entering the room, for example, tell the subject firmly which chair to take. Don't ever say "Find a seat." Giving the subject orders at intervals, if done in a low-key, firm way, maintains control by conditioning him to accept the interrogator's authority and dominance.

As the interrogation moves along, never show doubt or betray ignorance on any subject. The interrogator is in control, and this is the key to maintaining an air of confidence. If the subject asks a question which you can't answer, be firm in your reply: "We'll get to that a little later."

A stronger way would be to say, "I'm asking the questions here," but this would seem abrasive if the relationship hasn't deteriorated yet. Maintaining an air of friendliness without excessive familiarity helps the situation.2 The reason for not fraternizing with the subject is that "street-smart" offenders often interpret kindness as weakness.

Building rapport is the beginning. Keeping it, and adapting to changing needs, requires vigilance from the interrogator. He must think on several levels while asking his questions, and must always be aware of the need to adapt his tactics to the moment. Using good interrogating tactics is the follow-up to building rapport.

Sources

1. *The Manipulated Mind*, Denise Winn, London, The Octagon Press, 1983, pp. 114-115.

2. *The Gentle Art of Interviewing and Interrogation* Robert F. Royal and Steven R. Schutt, Englewood Cliffs, New Jersey, Prentice-Hall, Publishers, 1976, p. 119.

INTERROGATION TACTICS

Using the appropriate tactics can make or break an interrogation. It's important to plan the tactics before starting the session because improvisation will almost always be necessary during an interrogation. An improvisation often means a change of direction, which makes it important to have a basic plan as a guide. Planning also involves preparation, such as locale and rapport.

Interrogation techniques evolved in a loose manner, being passed by word of mouth, and from one generation of police to the next. These techniques and tactics are based on what we can call "practical psychology," not laboratory experiments or academic theories. This is fortunate, because American psychology got sidetracked by Freudian theories for several decades, and if the police had followed in step, interrogation would have become a dying craft.

American methods are loosely based on British ones, with regard for the "rights" of the suspects. The emphasis is on establishing rapport with the suspect and encouraging him to relieve his emotional tension by confiding in the interrogator, and making a confession. Various emotional ploys come into the picture, such as the tired old "good guy - bad guy" routine.

MIRANDA: INS AND OUTS

Timing of the interrogation is vital. So is the subject's status. If the interrogation is that of a suspect who isn't under arrest, he's free to get up and leave when he wishes. On the other hand, arresting the subject means that it's necessary to "read him his rights" as soon as possible after the arrest. In practice, this usually means at the scene of the arrest, as soon as the subject is handcuffed and searched.

Inexperienced investigators sometimes arrest a subject prematurely, feeling pressured to do this to prevent escape, or to establish on paper that they're "doing something" regarding the case. Because arrest requires the arresting officer to furnish the arrestee a copy of the warrant, if there is one, to state the charge to the accused, and to advise him of his rights, it's a definite turning point in the investigation.

Arrest is essential in certain types of crimes. A violent crime in which the officer intervenes and captures the suspect requires arrest on the spot. Other types of investigations furnish no such pressure because it's likely that the suspect(s) will try to escape. By playing his cards close to his vest, the investigating officer can prevent a suspect's knowing how heavy is the suspicion on him. It may be desirable to lull a subject, not allowing him to know how closely the investigation's come to focus upon him, in order to get more information out of him in interrogation sessions. Not alarming him also lessens the chance that he'll decide to flee. Delaying arrest can provide an opportunity to interrogate a subject without advising him of his rights, without having his attorney present, and without informing him of the exact charges.

There can be powerful pressures to coerce cooperation from a subject prior to arrest. If the case is one of employee theft, even the most dull-witted person must realize that refusing to "cooperate" will jeopardize his employment. In other instances, it's obvious that cooperation with the investigator tends to give the appearance of innocence, of "having nothing to hide." In many instances, this can be exploited to delve into matters that have nothing to do with the current investigation, and which would be disallowed after arrest. The subject, if he's eager to please, will furnish information willingly, especially on topics that don't pose the danger of implicating him.

This can be far-reaching. An investigation into company theft, for example, can broaden into exploring the extent of drug use among employees. It's often possible to coerce a subject into revealing information that he feels won't harm himself and yet will tend to "get him off the hook." Without the constraints dictated by the laws covering arrest and suspects' rights, the investigation can be free-wheeling and far-reaching.

It's preferable to read the suspect his "Miranda rights" in front of another officer if possible. This is especially important if there's more than one arrestee. A court is more likely to believe two officers together than one if there's an allegation that the arrestee did not receive his rights. The exact wording of the "rights card" varies from one locale to another, but roughly it says this:

"You have the right to remain silent.

"Anything you say can be used against you in a court of law.

"You have the right to have an attorney present before questioning and to be with you during questioning, if you so desire. If you cannot afford an attorney you have the right to have an attorney appointed for you before questioning.

"Do you understand these rights?

"Will you voluntarily answer my questions?"

Some jurisdictions issue "Miranda cards" to officers to read to arrestees. Others issue cards with a line for the suspect and the officer to sign, to denote the reading and understanding of the rights. This avoids doubt that the suspect was advised of his rights.

Getting around the requirement of the Miranda Warning is a technique in its own right. American police have developed methods of adhering to the letter of the judicial requirement strictly, while in fact circumventing it.[1] Officers can read the warning in an off-hand manner, conveying by their attitude that it's only a formality and actually meaningless. In other instances, an officer will perjure himself that he gave the Miranda Warning.[2] An important point to consider is whether to tape-record the interrogation with the Miranda Warning included. There are good reasons for taping an interrogation, and the officer must take into account the effect in court if he omits Miranda or delivers it in a manner that negates its importance.

Lessening the impact of the Miranda Warning requires some salesmanship, because it's necessary to "sell" the subject the idea that ignoring or giving up his rights will gain him more than utilizing them. One way to do this is to play heavily on the "innocent people have nothing to hide" theme. Telling the subject repeatedly that silence is evidence of guilt may break him down. What aids this is the simple, practical fact that guilt is often decided in the police station as much as in the court. Despite the way the law reads, with a presumption of innocence until proven guilty, most people, including suspects, don't think that way. There's usually an unspoken, but underlying assumption that the police wouldn't arrest anyone unless they felt he were guilty. The reason that this belief is so wide-spread is that it's true. The police generally don't try to "frame" purely innocent people. When they arrest someone, it's because they feel not only that he's guilty, but that they can make a case. The atmosphere in the police station aids this assumption, and it's easy for an interrogator to argue convincingly (because he believes it) that an innocent person is cooperative with the police.

"Look, you've got your rights, and you can have a lawyer if you want one. Nobody here's going to try to take your rights away from you. The Captain wouldn't allow that, anyway. But put yourself in my shoes. I just arrested you, and here you are, telling me that you're innocent. You say you're innocent, but you can't tell me where you were on the night it happened. What am I supposed to think? What would you think? See what I mean? Now think hard about this, too. What would a jury think?"

An appeal of this nature sometimes works in persuading a subject to avoid insisting on his Miranda Rights. If the interrogator delivers it convincingly and forcefully, he's got the best possible opportunity for effect immediately after reciting the Miranda Warning, because the police station is not a court-room, and the subject is for the moment isolated from familiar and/or helpful persons. Success in persuading the subject will prolong the isolation.

Having gotten the subject of the Miranda Warning out of the way, let's consider some mythology that has sprung up. Aubry and Caputo claim that

American police officers don't try to use tactics that confuse the subject to get a confession. Their viewpoint is that the police always play by the rules, and adhere closely to the law and sound criminal investigation practice.3

CONFESSIONS: THE REAL STORY

This is the official presentation, and isn't quite accurate. In reality, police officers often use whatever it takes to obtain information or a confession. This doesn't mean that American police are brutes, as police interrogators all over the world use similar tactics. The trend has been away from physical punishment, mainly because the courts have restrained the police by disallowing coerced confessions. Additionally, a police officer opens himself to both civil and criminal liability if he tortures a suspect. It's still difficult to prove that a suspect was tortured, and more difficult yet to convict an officer, but it takes only one instance to sink an officer's entire career.

Psychological coercion, on the other hand, leaves no cuts or bruises that can show in court. This is why it's in common use. We find Aubry and Caputo citing an example of psychological coercion by an interrogator later in their book.4

Let's also dispose of another official myth, that of the voluntary confession obtained because of a deeply-ingrained "need to confess."5 In separating fact from fiction, let's list the reasons, both practical and intangible, that lead suspects to confess.

1. Some want to relieve guilt. This only happens with some situational offenders, not career criminals or sociopaths. The hard cases don't feel guilt.6

2. Some subjects confess to relieve the anxiety. Being captive without knowing what the future holds produces anxiety, and confessing can resolve the situation and remove doubts.

3. Some confess to relieve the discomfort of psychological pressure by the interrogator. This is a common reason, and one that works against even hardened criminals. Hard and relentless interrogation can fatigue even the most determined suspect and induce a confession.

4. Some confess to stop the pain of torture. As we'll see, physical torture is alive and well in the United States.

5. Finally, some confess as the result of a "deal." In many instances, rational and practical factors determine the outcome. When the physical or eyewitness evidence is overwhelming, it's reasonable to admit guilt and throw oneself on the mercy of the police. In other instances, the "deal" involves treachery. A suspect agrees to "turn over" his friends or associates in return for a reduction or dismissal of charges.

DECIDING THE DIRECTION

The interrogator, while working on establishing rapport, has had a chance to "size up" the subject. He has also had a chance to glean information from the subject's "record," or "yellow sheet," if he has one. This is probably one of the more valuable tools available to the investigator. The much-vaunted "intuitive" ability which some investigators have in detecting untruth probably has a lot to do with scrutinizing the subject's history and forming obvious judgments from that.

This discussion will center around having only one or two interrogators present. There's no need for more, and the atmosphere of confidence, if attainable, becomes impaired with too many people in the room.7 One extraordinary example of this was the bungled interrogation of Lee Harvey Oswald after the shooting of President Kennedy. Instead of one or two, many people crowded into the small room. There were, according to the Warren Report, the police officer guarding Oswald, several Dallas detectives, and representatives from other agencies. These included the U.S. Secret Service, the FBI, the U.S. Marshall's Office, and even one Postal Inspector, coincidentally named "Holmes." Nobody thought to bring a tape recorder, which is why the record of this important interrogation is incomplete. In any event, with a crowd in the room, a coherent interrogation becomes impossible. There's a tendency for several officers to ask questions at once, and this leads to working at cross-purposes.

Once the interrogator has established rapport with the suspect, he can begin the main body of the interrogation. At this point the suspect doesn't know what the interrogator knows, which creates an aura of uncertainty. This simple fact forces a decision at the outset. The interrogator must decide whether it's best to lay his cards on the table or to keep the subject guessing. If the evidence against the suspect is conclusive, and will stand up in court, the interrogator may decide to lay it out point by point, to convince the suspect that resistance is useless. If the case is complete, however, what's the use of obtaining a confession? There's no need for input from the suspect to carry the case to a successful conclusion.

The answer lies in the collateral benefits of interrogation. With the suspect neatly wrapped up,

73

there may still be some loose ends. The proceeds of the crime may not yet be recovered. If there were accomplices, the police may not know their identities or locations.

Without a case that the interrogator can make appear conclusive, he must choose another approach. Keeping the suspect guessing is valuable because it has several advantages.

1. The suspect doesn't know how weak the case against him is. This leaves him vulnerable to a bluff, if the interrogator so chooses.

2. The uncertainty helps build anxiety, which fatigues the suspect and lowers his resistance.

3. Not knowing what the interrogator knows tends to keep the suspect's replies truthful, and gives the interrogator an edge. By mixing questions to which he knows the answers with those to which he doesn't, the interrogator can keep a running check on whether the subject's giving him the straight story.

If necessary, the interrogator can specify exactly what the charges are against the suspect. This probably will have already been covered by the arresting officer, since court decisions have held that the arrestee must be informed of the charge against him. As a practical matter, if the arrest was flagrante delicto, without a warrant, the suspect knows. If it was a warrant service, the information would be on the warrant, of which the suspect gets a copy at the time of arrest.

Some interrogators prefer to soften the subject up with the "silent treatment" before starting the interrogation. Bringing him into the room and having him sit down while the interrogator reads his file is one way. Another is for the interrogator to tell the suspect that he's not interested in hearing fabrications, only the truth, and to refrain from speaking unless he's prepared to be truthful.

Because many people are habituated to speaking or listening, and not having long periods of silence, this sometimes works. It can also work with a subject who's not too swift mentally. We must anticipate, however, that most people will be sophisticated enough not to be vulnerable to this ploy.

A good way to move into the topic of interest without being heavy-handed is for the interrogator to say something like this: "There have been certain accusations made against you. I'd like to give you a chance to tell your side of the story."

This implies more than it says. It suggests that the interrogator is on the suspect's side, eagerly offering him an opportunity to present "his side." This is a bit of salesmanship, because the suggestion that the interrogator's on the suspect's side is utterly misleading but hard to pin down and prove false. Even if there's a taped record of the interrogation, the interrogator will come out appearing to be fair-minded rather than deceptive.

ELICITING THE SUSPECT'S STORY

With a subject willing to talk, it's best to follow the same plan as with an interview with a witness. The interrogator should encourage the subject to tell the story in his own way and in his own words. This is the free-form narrative, and during this the interrogator should be attentive and encouraging. It's critically important that the interrogator not display, by word, manner, or expression, that he disbelieves anything the subject says.8 This gives the subject enough rope to hang himself, if he so chooses.

Direct Questioning

Once the subject's related his account, it's time for direct examination to bring out additional information that he may not have covered. In this stage, the interrogator's still fishing, and he should be positive and supportive, still encouraging the subject to say what he wishes. The interrogator should, however, mix questions about matters he knows with others relating to those he doesn't know. This gives him an immediate check on the subject's truthfulness.

A good reason for making a record of some sort, either written or taped, is to have the subject's allegations down for later checking. Some assertions may be false, and need checking out. Others are useful in evidence or as investigative leads, but they still need the same checking out.

Cross-examination

The last stage is cross-examination, which is basically an adversary proceeding. This is when the interrogator scrutinizes omissions and discrepancies. He puts on the pressure to elicit complete and truthful answers. If the subject's not forthcoming, he points this out, and requests better cooperation if the subject hopes to clear himself.

If the interrogator doesn't like an answer at this point, he can show his disapproval by a raised eyebrow. Another technique is to repeat a word from the subject's answer, but with a questioning note. If the subject says, for example, "I came directly home," and the interrogator suspects that he stopped along the way, he can repeat to the subject, "Directly?"

If the interrogator's purpose is to elicit more information, and he wishes to keep the emotional tension low in order not to risk alienating the subject, he has to handle lies and omissions carefully. He should never refer to them as what they are, but instead use neutral language such as "points" and "problem areas." A way to handle a lie is to say, "I have trouble with this point. What, exactly, did you mean when you said that - - - - -?"

Unless and until the gloves come off, the interrogator should use face-saving ways to point out the subject's lies and omissions. Asking "Are you sure about that?" or saying "Perhaps you made a mistake." or "Maybe you meant something else." are ways of contradicting a suspect while minimizing the chances of his taking offense.

If the interrogator senses that he's facing a resistant subject, he may decide to use a sales technique known as "taking the wind out of his sails." This is anticipating objections, stating them, and countering them before asking the subject to speak. An illustration of how the technique works is in the following imaginary example:

"Okay, now let's get down to a few problem areas. You know that I need to know where you were when this happened. Maybe you're gonna tell me that you were with your girl friend at that time. I know her, and I know that she'd back up anything you might say, so I'm not gonna take her seriously. You might also tell me that you were out of town, but unless you can show me a bill from a hotel, I'm not gonna buy that. Don't even think of telling me that you were laid up in a hospital. I'll just laugh because you don't look like you've been ill."

This example contained several types of rebuttals. One was an outright attack on the credibility of an alibi witness. Another was conditional, a refusal to accept an alibi unless the subject could produce supporting evidence. The third was a dismissal of an unlikely alibi precisely because the subject's physical state ruled it out.

PERSUADING THE SUBJECT TO TALK

A difficulty can arise if the subject's reluctant to talk. This requires the interrogator to use his manipulative skills. There are ways to appeal to the subject. One is to tell him that the evidence already available is adequate, and that what may make the difference between going to trial or not is the subject's cooperation. "If you've got nothing to hide, tell me about it. If you don't want to talk to me, it looks like you're trying to cover something up."

This is one of many ways to mobilize the subject's anxiety. Getting an interrogation to succeed takes salesmanship in many instances. The interrogator must "sell" the subject on the idea that opening up is better than keeping silent. This can be made to work despite the Miranda Warning, as we've already noted. The Miranda Warning takes only a couple of minutes, at most. This satisfies the legal requirement, giving the interrogator hours to work on the subject to counter the effect.

One way to persuade the subject to talk is to refer to his guilt. This only works with situational offenders, though. A vehicular homicide suspect is probably remorseful, and telling him that he'll feel better after talking about it may overcome his reluctance to testify against himself.

A hard case is still open to a variant of this appeal. Saying that confessing will release him from the anxiety of uncertainty can have a powerful appeal. These people don't have active consciences, but their senses of self-preservation and self-interest are alive and well. An offender may well prefer knowing what's going to happen to him to digging in his heels and leaving the issue still in doubt.

Sympathy

The interrogator assumes an attitude of sympathetic understanding of the suspect's situation. To encourage him to talk, he may say, "Sure, I know how it is. I would have done the same thing in your shoes." This is the sort of tactic that will work against a man who's killed his wife, but not a professional criminal.

There are several variants of the sympathy approach. One is to tell the subject that his actions are understandable because the temptation was too much. This implies that anyone in his position might have done what he did. This works only in cases of material gain. Other types of cases require a little more polishing of the approach.

"What will your family think?" is another sympathy approach. Here the interrogator urges the suspect to unburden himself so that his family may be reassured. This implies a faith in the essential goodness of the suspect, which may not at all be true.

Another way, closely related to the other "sympathy" approaches, is to tell the subject: "Anyone would have done what you did." This is applicable in cases of domestic violence, for example. Suggesting to the subject that his situation was intolerable, and that anyone else would have also resorted to violence is a purely emotional appeal, an intimation that the interrogator understands and forgives him, even though the court might not. However, we steer carefully away from that topic during this interrogation.

Another variant on this theme is to shift the blame to the victim. Pretend that the subject was provoked beyond resistance, and that the real guilt lies with the victim for provoking him. Again, we make no mention of how the law really reads, but pretend to absolve him within the confines of the interrogation room.

Minimizing the crime is yet another way to reassure the subject. Telling him that you've seen far worse, that his offense is so common that it barely deserves attention, is a way of persuading him that there's no need for concealment. There are other variants on the theme of minimizing the crime that we'll cover in the next section, the one dealing with deception.

"We know all about it."

Telling a suspect that other evidence points to his guilt sometimes works in obtaining a confession. Officers who try this often use a mixture of truth and bluff, to obtain the complete story. The most important ingredients in this sort of affair are a convincing manner and a credulous suspect. The obvious question, to any suspect who stops to think about it, is "If you know the whole story already, why do you need to ask me?"

DECEPTIONS

"We already have the evidence to convict you."

This is the basic falsification, and it can lead to many, many variants. It's necessary to adapt this story to the individual case, to each type of crime. In one instance, saying that eyewitness testimony places him at the crime scene may be enough to break him. In another, it might be necessary to show him a "statement" signed by a "witness" that states the suspect was indeed at the scene of the crime.

Another variation might be to have another officer or a friend play the role of "eyewitness." The role-player enters the room and goes through the charade of making an oral "statement" to the interrogator, who then tells him or her to return to the outer office to make a formal statement.

Still another ploy is the fake "line-up." This is the most elaborate of all, and requires cooperation from as many as a dozen participants. One or more "eyewitnesses" pick the subject out of a "line-up," conducted exactly as a real one would be except for the collusion.

Still another way of manufacturing "evidence" to coerce a confession is the fake phone call. If there's a telephone in the interrogation room, it can ring, by pre-arrangement, and the interrogator lifts the handpiece to take a "call" from the next room. He listens and makes comments which suggest that he's speaking with the crime lab. After hanging up, he informs the suspect, as if he hadn't been listening to every word, that the crime lab called to say that the fingerprints on the gun match his, etc.

Another way to structure this theme, if there's no phone in the room, is to have the interrogator called out to take a "phone call." After waiting outside for a couple of minutes, he returns to inform the suspect that the lab test came back positive, or whatever.

Still another way, in order not to lose continuity, is for another officer to come in with either a verbal or written message from the "crime lab," or a "coroner's report."

Off The Record

Asking the subject to tell the interrogator something in confidence may work. It may succeed at the outset, with a dull-witted subject, or it may work after a long and grueling session when both parties are tired and not at their best. One excellent ploy is to turn off the tape recorder on the table, if there is one, and tell the subject that his comments will be "off the record." At the end of the session, the recorder may be out of tape. The interrogator makes a big show of relaxing, perhaps fishing out a cigarette and also offering one to the suspect. His attitude conveys the message, "Now that that's over, let's relax for a couple of minutes." There are several ways to try to get the subject to open up:

"Off the record, weren't you worried that your partner might be tempted to run out on you, since he held the money?"

"What do you think's gonna happen when your partner comes in here to spend a few hours with me? How long you think he can hold out?"

"Weren't you worried that the woman might scream?"

"Ever shoot anybody before?"

"How did you get away with it for so long?"

"I could never understand how you managed to pull the job off by yourself."

All of these introductory statements are strong lead-ins to the off-the-record session. A variant is to share a meal with the subject, exploiting the opportunity for small talk and gradually leading him around to the topic of interest. This works well if the interrogation has been tense. This makes the subject vulnerable to the let-down that accompanies the release of pressure.[9]

Fatigue can also play a role. A way to prompt the expression of fatigue is to call for a break. Letting the subject relax for a few minutes, while the interrogator talks about something else with him or his partner, can lead to a lulling of the defenses. It also leads to an increase in suggestibility.[10]

This can take several forms. It can make the subject more vulnerable to a deception, such as the one that his partner's confessed. It can also lead the subject to accept an "off-the-record" assertion, either expressed or just implied by the relaxed atmosphere of the break.

Controlling the pace of the interrogation is a vital part of the effort. There are several principles at work here, and the interrogator must understand exactly what he's doing, and why, for this to give him the optimum benefits. As a start, the interrogator asks the questions, and calls for breaks and meals. The subject must never be allowed to have anything he requests right away. Even a toilet call must be delayed for a few minutes, while the interrogator and the subject "clear up a few points." This is to continue the conditioning that the interrogator has absolute power over the subject. If the subject has cigarettes, he must not be allowed to smoke without permission, and one effective way of doing this is to have him empty his pockets and hand everything over before the start of the session.

Denying or delaying breaks, smokes, and toilet calls are ways of building discomfort and tension. While this denying must not go so far as to be excessively cruel, with discretion denying can be very effective in building the proper atmosphere and conditioning the subject.

Metering out stress and fatigue makes the subject more eager to take a break when the interrogator decides. This increases his vulnerability to the ploys mentioned above.

Minimizing The Crime

There are many ways to do this by outright deception. One factor in the interrogator's favor is the suspect's limited knowledge of the law and the criminal justice system. Another is his willingness to believe what he wants to hear. Despite having a lot of "street smarts," many suspects are open to this sort of deception, which is probably under-exploited by American police officers. A final factor in the interrogator's favor is the subject's isolation, if he's managed to keep it tight.

Withholding the news that the victim has died is one way of keeping the suspect from knowing that he's facing a "heavy" charge. One who thinks that he's up for "only" a lesser, non-capital offense won't be as much on his guard as the one who knows that it's a capital matter. The success of this ploy depends utterly on the interrogator's managing the news that the subject hears.

Another way to minimize the crime is to cite statutes and penalties falsely to convince the subject that his crime is not as severe as he might have thought. If the subject is a "jailhouse lawyer," bluffing him that the law was changed the previous week or month may work. A convincing manner is the key to this deception.

Another way, which can work very well for lesser crimes such as trespassing, shoplifting, and even burglary and assault, is to tell the subject that the victim may drop the charges. One way is to say: "Look, Mr. Moloney isn't a bad guy. He was in the choir with my brother. He knows you're just a young guy, and he told me that if you seem to show an understanding that you did wrong, he might drop the charges. What am I gonna tell him?"

Another way, for older offenders: "Look, Moloney knows that he lost his temper, and that he shouldn't have yelled at you that way. I talked with him and told him that I would have hit him if he'd given me that sort of mouth. I told him I could understand why you set the fire. He's gotta go on a trip next week, and doesn't like the idea of having to cancel out. He just might be ready to drop the charges. Now, if I can tell him that you confessed, said that you're sorry, and want to shake hands over it, I think I can get him to go for it."

Minimizing the consequences can also work. Incredibly, there are some people who are so hopeful that they'll believe the most ridiculous assertions. It's important to keep an ear wide open for a hint that a subject might be of this sort. One who's stolen from his employer might ask the interrogator if this means that he'll lose his job. An interrogator who's quick on his feet may answer that it may not necessarily happen, and that a good recommendation from him might persuade the employer to keep him on. Of course, this would depend on how forthcoming the subject is about the details of the offense. This will work if the subject's primed to believe it.

"Your Partner Confessed."

If there are multiple suspects, one major objective is to split them up, physically and psychologically. It's a cardinal error to allow them to share the same holding cell, even for a few minutes. It's best to keep them totally out of sight of each other, to prevent coordination of stories or even simple moral support. The easy part about isolating suspects from each other is that it's perfectly legal.

Splitting the bond between confederates is vital because driving a wedge between them allows the interrogator to exploit the weakest one, and to also make the others less secure.11 A way to do this is to reinforce any suspicions or doubts expressed by the subject. Creating doubts also helps in the attempt to break the collective bond. In attempting this, it's helpful to know the histories of the people involved. One suspect, for example, might have a record of residence in a foreign country. If he's the one not yet caught, suggesting to the subject that perhaps he fled and abandoned him to his fate can impair his morale. If he's already "ratted" on an accomplice in a previous crime, this can be very convincing. Sometimes, fabrication may be necessary.

Convincing a subject that his partner already confessed and implicated him has a couple of variants. The subject may even disclose facts previously unsuspected by the police. A suspect bent on revenge on a perfidious partner may disclose that his partner has not only confessed, but has shifted the main blame onto him. In a robbery, the driver can be told that his partner claimed that he did the shooting. This may provoke an angry denial, which sets the stage for the interrogator's saying, "If that's not true, then tell me what really happened."

"You're In For Murder!"

This can be useful in persuading a suspect to confess a lesser crime. A burglar, for example, can have this accusation thrown at him: "Just before the patrol-car officer caught you, a convenience store was knocked over a few blocks away. The guy who did it shot and killed the clerk. The coroner says it was a .38, just like yours. I think I've got my suspect, sitting right here!"

The suspect may willingly confess to the burglary to get off the hook with the murder charge. The "murder" can be a figment of the investigator's imagination.

FACTS TO WITHHOLD

In every investigation, there's a category of facts known as "investigative keys." These are facts about the crime which only the victim and the perpetrator can know, and which the investigator doesn't disclose to the press. It's important to keep certain facts about the crime closely held, because they provide checks on the validity of testimony.

There are occasionally people who seem guilty by their manner, or by the circumstances. There are also compulsive "confessors," mentally ill people who present themselves and offer to confess after a sensational crime. Not being able to relate the "guilty knowledge" when questioned is an indication that the subject's not guilty.

Choosing the investigative keys varies with each type of offense. In a property crime, the exact list of property missing is such an investigative key. A burglary or robbery that involves money provides an obvious detail to withhold — the exact amount missing. Sex crimes provide excellent opportunities because of certain bizarre features, such as tying up the victim, the brand of lubricant used, if any, and the exact sequence of acts committed by the offender.

There can arise problems with these investigative keys. One relates to the amount stolen in a property crime. Some victims declare more than they actually lost, in an effort to get larger insurance settlements. An investigator with a suspect who claims to have stolen less than officially declared faces a touchy problem. He must resolve this because the discrepancy might harm the case. One way is to return to the victim and suggest that his original report might have been in error. This is a quick and face-saving way to do it, especially if the investigator explains to the victim that in the stress of a crime, many victims make similar "errors."

Another way is to claim that the suspect did commit the crime, but isn't candid about the amount he stole. Juries are often prepared to believe this if the amount is substantial and the prosecutor convinces them that suspect is withholding it as a nest egg for when he's released from prison. It may also result in a longer sentence than otherwise.

Other problems that can arise are leaking the details of the guilty knowledge, either because of a slip by the police or because the real perpetrator has talked about his act to the subject in custody. These can lead to false confessions.

TACTICS ARE IMPORTANT

Using the proper tactics is vital to a successful interrogation. The interrogator should recognize, however, that he won't always be successful. This is because practically nothing works in real life as it appears on the printed page. There are many books on interrogation which lay out procedures with the unstated implication that following these will inevitably produce the desired results. The reader will be disappointed.

The value of tactics is that they work most of the time. Even when there's a failure, correct tactics minimize the failure and provide room to recuperate, regroup, and take the initiative once more. Most importantly, a set of tactics provides a framework upon which to build an investigative plan.

Sources

1. *The Mugging,* Morton Hunt, New York, Signet Books, 1972, pp. 121-122.

2. *Ibid.,* p. 227.

3. *Criminal Interrogation,* Arthur S. Aubry, Jr., and Rudolph R. Caputo, Springfield, Illinois, Charles C. Thomas, Publisher, 1980, p. xi.

4. *Ibid.,* pp. 226-227.

5. *Ibid.,* pp. 41-46. This is a self-serving chapter which explains away confessions by ascribing them to an innate pressure within soul, or some such. It's a convenient explanation, one which allows leaving untouched the uncomfortable subject of rigorous methods of coercive interrogations.

6. A good example of this was the reply given by a con artist to the question: "Aren't you sorry for what you did?" The con artist replied: "I'm sorry I got caught, if that's what you mean."

7. *Criminal Interrogation,* p. 186.

8. *Telling Lies,* Paul Ekman, New York, W.W. Norton & Company, 1985, p. 182. The value of letting the suspect present his story uninterrupted first is generally recognized by authorities. We find the same advice in *The Gentle Art of Interviewing and Interrogation,* Robert F. Royal and Steven R. Schutt, Englewood Cliffs, New Jersey, Prentice-Hall, 1976, p. 120.

9. *The Gentle Art of Interviewing and Interrogation*, Robert F. Royal and Steven R. Schutt, Englewood Cliffs, New Jersey, Prentice-Hall, 1976, p. 77.

10. *Ibid.*, p. 76.

11. *Ibid.*, p. 82.

TACTICS, PART II: CONSOLIDATING THE INTERROGATION

At some point in many criminal interrogations, there is a relaxation of defenses by the subject, a surrender, which some authorities call the "breakthrough."[1] This may come suddenly, when the subject can't take the pressure anymore, or when the interrogator exposes a major lie which destroys his entire story. It can also come gradually, a result of a conscious decision by the subject.

The sudden and dramatic success can come with a subject who's not very self-possessed, and who is easily surprised and disconcerted by a definitive contradiction of his version of the facts by the interrogator. This amounts to an intellectual triumph by the interrogator, and although dramatic, doesn't happen very often. However, the interrogator should not abandon hope of this sudden "breakthrough," even though it's rare. The groundwork necessary to attain this sort of victory is the same required to consolidate the results of any interrogation. It consists of the same thorough, tedious, recording of the facts and collection of physical evidence as is necessary to bring any case to a successful conclusion. The interrogator must cross-check the subject's account with the known facts, and return to the subject's previous statements to examine them for serious inconsistencies and contradictions.

Sometimes a small detail isn't conclusive at all, but alerts the interrogator to the possibility of a major lie. For example, a subject who claims to have been in a certain city at a certain time as an alibi may misstate a minor fact about that city, revealing his ignorance. If he doesn't know if the city has a subway system, or where the airport is, there's reason to suspect that he's never been there. By itself, this lack of knowledge isn't conclusive, but if the interrogator presses the subject for additional details which he can't furnish, the breakthrough may come.

DOCUMENTATION

Also important is the donkey work of verifying assertions through seeking documentation. Simple pieces of paper such as hotel and car rental receipts can provide important leads. A charge card slip can place the subject at a certain location on a certain date, and checking out the vendor's records may even permit establishing the time. Confronting the subject with these can have a profound impact because of the special status of something that's on paper. If it's written, it must be true.

INDICATORS OF SURRENDER

The interrogator may also notice symptoms of a readiness to come to an accommodation by the subject. A subject who asks a hypothetical question about the possibility of a "deal" shows that he's at least thinking about it. This probing may come from a street-smart subject or from a naive one, but it's an opportunity for the interrogator to encourage a surrender. There are several important points to watch about replying to such a probe:

1. The street-smart suspect may be seeking the best deal for himself, even if this involves betraying his accomplices. Because he's utterly immoral about this, and fundamentally feels no loyalty towards them, the prospects for the interrogator are better than with other types of subjects. It only works if he knows how to exploit the opportunity.

2. The street-smart suspect is almost certainly not going to "deal" fairly if the interrogator allows him to get away with anything. He may easily hold back some information for later trading with a prosecutor. It's vital for the interrogator to remember that his suspect is a criminal who habitually exploits relationships, and for whom "fairness" is a foreign concept. This is why the interrogator must avoid making any premature commitments. The way to handle a request for a deal is to be as non-commital as possible, emphasizing to the suspect that it's impossible to pin down the details of the deal until the interrogator knows what the subject has to offer:

SUSPECT: "If I can give you some names, what kind of deal can I get?"

INTERROGATOR: "That depends on the names, and how they check out. I'd also like to hear what else you have to offer."

SUSPECT: "I need to know what I can get before I start giving anything away to you."

INTERROGATOR: "I can't make any promises until I know what you've got to give me. I also need to check it out."

This is the one point which is absolutely non-negotiable, and the interrogator must dig in his heels and resist every effort by the suspect to persuade him to make a premature commitment.

3. The interrogator's on safe ground in standing by his refusal. This is because both he and the suspect

tacitly recognize certain unwritten rules. One is that the suspect is a criminal, and in his position might say anything to "get off the hook." That makes the interrogator's need to verify the suspect's information logical and legitimate. Another rule is that the interrogator's not the final authority in most cases. He has to work a deal through his superiors, and perhaps the prosecutor's office. Finally, the suspect will tend to trust the interrogator because he must. This brings us back to the mechanism of the lie that is believed because the victim has a deep need to believe it. The suspect needs the deal. This is true whether the interrogator is sincere and trustworthy or not. He must accept the interrogator's condition to lay out his offering without knowing what it's worth because the alternative is worse. At least, here he has a chance to get a reduced sentence.

4. The request for a deal puts the interrogator in the top position of the power relationship. All relationships involve power, with the person who needs it more holding the submissive position. The person who needs it less is dominant. In an interrogation, the interrogator is not as dominant as he could be, because of his great need for information. This is true despite his holding the subject in a weak position, such as arrest.

In the request for a deal, the suspect has indicated a need, and shown that he wants it more than the interrogator, reversing the power relationship. He shows the need, which the interrogator is in a position to satisfy or deny. This is why the interrogator can now press the subject hard, and obtain compliance, whereas he could not before. For example, he can now insist that the suspect put his statement in writing. The suspect can't easily refuse without provoking an accusation of insincerity or non-cooperation. The interrogator can badger the suspect, asking, "Is that all there is?" at intervals, or telling the suspect, "You've got to do better than that."

NAILING IT DOWN

With everything down on paper, the interrogator can begin the task of coordinating the efforts to exploit the "breakthrough." This may involve a supplementary investigation if the suspect was able to provide information on other crimes or other suspects.

The suspect must have provided the investigator what he needs before any discussion of the details of the deal can take place. The minimum is a signed statement or confession. This can be from a standard framework provided by the prosecutor's office. The reason for a standard form is to satisy certain legal requirements. All confessions today have a paragraph at the beginning stating that the confession is freely given, and that the subject has not been coerced. The paragraph also states that the subject had been advised of his constitutional rights, such as the right to remain silent, and the right to an attorney. It goes on to say that the subject waives his rights in making the statement. The subject also acknowledges that he knows that his statement may be used against him in a court of law. It also states that the subject is confessing without the influence of any promises by the authorities. These are white lies, and everyone knows they are. However, they satisfy the legal requirements of our hypocritical system.

They are also "overkill," because the legal requirements are not always that extensive to validate or admit a confession. The interrogator must, however, try to cover all of the contingencies because although a confession may be valid at the time it is taken, a change in requirements, brought about by new legislation or a court decision, may make it invalid.

Because the confessed suspect knows that the deal depends on the accuracy of his material, it's possible to delay gratification while the investigators check it out. This may take days or weeks, and although the suspect may become impatient, there's nothing he can do. Once the statements are on paper, with the standard disclaimer that they were freely given in full knowledge of his rights, they're fairly solid and hard to negate. If the suspect is still in custody, having been denied bail or release on his own recognizance, he's very much in the interrogator's power. This allows the interrogator to return to exploit the victory further. There's often a need for this, because not all details available are given by the suspect at the time of the initial statement.[2]

Cases tend to develop at their own speed, and much information is sequential. This means that it's not available until other information has come to light. Even the need for additional information may not be apparent until certain steps of an investigation have been completed.

In the case of our hypothetical suspect, he may have given information about his accomplice. Upon arrest, the accomplice provides information about another crime committed with the aid of a third party. The investigator will usually find it worthwhile to return to the first suspect to obtain any information he has about the third party. He'll also find it essential to cross-check the accomplice's statements with the first suspect. Additional information which requires more cross-checking with the first suspect may come to light. All of these developments will probably result in a long delay of the final settlement on the "deal." This is partly because it's undesirable to make the deal final until the interrogator's suspect is "milked dry." Under the influence of uncertainty, the suspect has an incentive to continue to cooperate. If the deal's final, he has nothing further to gain, and may decline cooperation.

There may be a temptation for the interrogator to renege on the deal. This could come about because the crime is so repulsive, or the suspect so revolting, that the interrogator feels he should get the maximum punishment. Such an attitude is human, but very unprofessional, because above all an interrogator must maintain his objectivity.

There are several negative consequences of reneging on a deal. The first is loss of credibility. It's impossible to keep a suspect totally incommunicado for an indefinite time, and sooner or later, he'll have contact with family, friends, an attorney, and fellow convicts. He'll spread the word about a deceitful interrogator, and this will sabotage any efforts to deal in the future. Although deceit is one of the interrogator's "stock-in-trades," the main point to deceit is not to get caught. An interrogator who breaks his word on a deal has exposed himself unequivocally.

Another important consequence of reneging on a deal may be a successful repudiation of the confession in court. Although the confession contains language that states that it was given voluntarily and without any trade-off, everyone knows that this is untrue. The white lies are accepted only as long as both parties agree to them. Moreover, everyone knows that confessions are exchanges for deals. A defense attorney may convince a court that the confession is invalid if the authorities renege on the deal.

A third consequence may be flight by the suspect. If the suspect's a situational offender, he may obtain release on bail or "ROR." Thus free, he may panic if the authorities break their promise to him. Because he's not a career criminal and a sociopath, faith in the "system" is important to him, and the belief that he'll be treated fairly in return for cooperation is the most important factor in his returning to face a court. Any breach of faith may easily result in his breaking away and evading the law.

Yet another effect has to do with the psychology of conditioning and its effect upon the suspect. Proper conditioning requires predictability. The suspect must know that certain of his actions will bring punishment and others will bring rewards. This is the basic framework for manipulating his behavior. Going back on a promise is an example of unpredictability which will upset the entire relationship and destroy all hope for future accommodations.

This is why it's important for an interrogator to follow a certain code of ethics, however crude it may be. The interrogator, as an authority figure, must represent a fixed point in a changing world in order to be effective.

Sources

1. *The Gentle Art of Interviewing and Interrogation,* Robert F. Royal and Steven R. Schutt, Englewood Cliffs, New Jersey, Prentice-Hall, 1976, pp. 143-151.

2. *Ibid.,* p. 149.

TECHNOLOGICAL METHODS

A recent news story concerned a polygraph examination and the effect it had on one of the most serious espionage cases in recent American history. An article appearing in the September 7, 1986, issue of the *Washington Post* stated that a polygraph test supposedly showed deception on the part of John Walker, convicted spy. It suggested that he wasn't cooperating with the government, as he claimed to be. One area of interest in the investigation was the number of people who took part in the spy ring, which penetrated the U.S. Navy's cryptographic secrets. That federal investigative agencies should become so concerned over the test results indicates one of two things. Either the polygraph is a reliable instrument, or the investigators are desperate. In this chapter, we'll scrutinize the polygraph and other technological innovations and try to find out how effective they really are.

20TH-CENTURY TECHNOLOGY

For understandable reasons, we've come to place a lot of reliance on scientific innovations. These have revolutionized transportation, communication, farming, and many other fields. Scientific crime detection, although not quite as effective as crime novel writers represent, has helped the criminal justice system greatly.

There have also been other developments which have not turned out as well. Those devised as aids to interrogation have been both controversial and unreliable. These have included the polygraph, or "lie detector," the voice stress analyzer, hypnotism, and various drugs.

Americans tend to be gadgeteers, and to place their faith in machines. Often, this is justifiable, but in some instances, the results are questionable. One disturbing aspect of this faith is that for some people, science has become a new religion, and they tend to believe anything presented to them in scientific trappings. Unfortunately, scientists are sometimes mistaken. In other instances, charlatans pass themselves off as scientists to gain credibility. It's hard to find a field in which science, quasi-science, and pseudo-science have had such influence as in interrogation.

Fiction and screen writers are also to blame. So are those who present sensationalized versions dressed up as "facts." They tend to assign popular names which suggest inaccuracies, such as "lie detector" and "truth serum." We'll look at these devices and drugs, and examine what they really do and don't do.

"LIE DETECTORS"

In this section, we'll consider both the polygraph and the devices which measure variations in the voice, because the basic theory under which they work is the same. We've seen in the section on psychology that stress produces certain physical symptoms. Among these are increased heart rate and respiration, increased muscular tension, and an increase in sweat secretion. There are other effects, such as an increase in adrenaline level in the blood. There is also an alleged change in voice undertones, which supposedly signals untruth.

The polygraph is a complex machine, which measures and records several physical symptoms simultaneously. Usually, it records blood pressure, pulse rate, respiration, and skin moisture. The amazing fact about this device is that it's built with 1930s technology.[1] Although there are newly-manufactured polygraphs, they still work the same way and don't reflect the scientific developments of the intervening years. Another amazing fact is that John Larson, one of its original developers, conducted a controlled test of its effectiveness before 1940 and found the polygraph to be hopelessly inaccurate. He denounced it as a "racket" and expressed regret for his role in its development and promotion.[2] In the years since, the courts have rarely admitted polygraph tests as evidence. In the few instances in which it has happened, the polygraph industry has publicized it forcefully as a sign of growing acceptance.

This is a critically important point. The polygraph, in various forms, has been with us since the 1920s. There have been, therefore, many decades for its promoters to prove the worth of the device in many courts here and abroad. Most of these efforts have met with failure at the same time that other scientific tools, such as voice-prints, laser questioned-document analysis, and various biomedical techniques were gaining acceptance.

The theory behind the polygraph is simple. A person who lies is under stress, and the polygraph detects this stress, thus revealing deception. The examiner compares the charted reactions to innocuous "control" questions with the ones to the

101

relevant questions. If the subject shows a higher pulse rate after being asked, "Did you murder your wife?" than he does when asked, "Is your name John Doe?", this is evidence of deception. There are many methods of asking the questions, in order to set up "control" questions. There are also variations, such as the "peak of tension test," but all depend on the subject's showing augmented responses to the significant questions.

There are at least two schools of thought regarding the interpretation of the results, which are displayed on a long strip of graph paper progressively unrolling from the machine as the device's pens record the subject's physical signs. One school maintains that the chart tells all, and that the examiner can tell whether the subject is truthful or deceptive by examining the squiggles. This implies that a qualified examiner should be able to read a chart and determine truth or deception without even seeing the subject. Few polygraph examiners go this far.

The other view is that "global scoring" is the better way. "Global scoring" means taking all factors into account. This is tacit recognition that the polygraph technique is a little weak, and that the examiner needs all the help he can get. He familiarizes himself with the facts of the case, to detect obvious flaws in the subject's account. He also notes the subject's manner, whether he's overly polite, hesitant, restless, avoiding eye contact, and other features of the subject's demeanor. Part of the procedure, if the charts don't reveal a strong "pattern" of lying, is to try to bluff the subject into thinking they do.

The problem with global scoring is that it depends very heavily on intuitive methods. Some examiners have a "knack" of ferreting out the truth, as some interrogators seem to have a talent for telling who's

102

lying in an interrogation. There are no mannerisms which unequivocally signal untruth.

Another prospect is that the examiner may let himself be influenced by subjective factors. If, for example, he examines several suspects in a case, all of whom deny complicity, he'll inevitably run into a subtle but definite influence which can warp his judgment. With the first suspects, he'll perhaps accept their denials. As he runs down the list, he'll realize that if all the previous suspects are innocent, one of the remainder must be guilty. He'll also feel the pressure to uncover the guilty party. He will, therefore, be less likely to believe the remaining suspects, whatever the evidence of the charts or the subject's mannerisms.

Reading the chart alone is weak. There are some measurably different physiological reaction patterns which differentiate between lie stress and that caused by other emotions. However, there's so much individual variation that a polygraph chart isn't a reliable indicator.

"Common sense" tells us that someone accused of a crime will be under stress from the accusation alone. If the subject's under arrest, separated from family and friends and locked up in a police station, the stress will be severe. The polygraph measures stress alone, without detecting the cause.

A subject hearing the question, "Did you murder your wife?", will have stress from any of several possible causes. One might be surprise, fear, or anger that he should be accused. Another could be grief at her death. Another possibility is anger at the actual murderer. All of these will make the polygraph jump.

The unfortunate fact is that there is no scientifically proven and consistent set of physiological responses that differentiate the truthful person from the liar.3 This is steadfastly denied by polygraph examiners.4

On the contrary, there are people who not only don't show stress when telling lies, but derive a positive pleasure from deception.5 It's naive to think that the liar is a scared, sniveling coward, bathed in anxiety over his deceptions. There are professional liars who enjoy deception, and even earn a living doing it. Salesmen are good examples. So are advertising people. Professional criminals and sociopaths are others, and these are the ones most likely to come into contact with the police.

Polygraph examiners sometimes try to justify their procedures by presenting statistics to uphold their claims. There have been various "studies" by polygraph examiners, most of them claiming success rates of 65% to 95%. This isn't as significant as it might seem. When there are only two choices, "truth" and "lie," chance alone dictates a success rate of 50%. Flipping a coin would give 50% accuracy.

There's also room for a little sleight-of-hand with the numbers. A polygraph examiner, evaluating 100 suspects, finds two deceptive. Only one, however, committed the crime. Does this mean that he's 98% or 99% accurate? Not at all. To get a valid figure, we have to calculate the percentage of true "hits," which is 1 out of 2, or 50%. This is what we'd expect from flipping a coin.

Still, polygraph technicians claim that their devices work, and often cite the number of confessions they've obtained from suspects as "proof." Actually, all this proves is that the threat of polygraph examination is intimidating to some suspects, and this is what induces them to confess.6 There have been some documented cases of false confessions being induced by severe interrogation techniques backed up by a polygraph examination given while the subject was physically and emotionally exhausted. In one such case, the subject, an 18-year-old boy, was accused of killing his mother, but denied even having been in the house when the crime occurred. Much later, a thorough investigation disclosed that his alibi was valid. However, at the moment he denied the crime to investigators, he submitted to a polygraph examination, which showed a strong stress pattern, and the interrogator convinced him that the polygraph couldn't be in error. He suggested that the boy was so guilt-ridden that he'd blanked the incident out of his mind.

Experienced lawbreakers, or those familiar with the polygraph and the tactics associated with it, would not be as vulnerable to this sort of treatment. Even a slight level of sophistication affords some power of resistance.

IS IT POSSIBLE TO FOOL THE POLYGRAPH?

There have been a number of ways suggested to "pass" the polygraph. These are in use by criminals and, surprisingly, many more honest people. One important reason for this is the abuse of the polygraph. Many employers use the "lie detector" to screen job applicants in ways that are not legitimate.

It's easy to understand that an employer wants applicants who don't have criminal records, especially if the position involves handling money or valuables. In view of the cost to employers when workers have alcohol or drug problems, it's also understandable that a personnel manager would want to screen these out. Some don't stop here, though. They want to pry into what most people would consider their private affairs. There may be questions regarding political beliefs, health history, financial affairs, and driving record.[7] In some instances, there will even be questions about sexual habits.[8] This is very much like the psychological tests some employers administer, in that there's a tinge of intellectual peeping-tomism.

This can be very dangerous for the applicant. Polygraph examiners state that about 75% of their subjects in pre-employment screenings make damaging admissions.[9] What makes it especially galling is the fiction that the candidate is taking the test "voluntarily."[10] The applicant is often required to sign a form stating that it is voluntary. Actually, the applicant knows that, while he doesn't have to take the test, the employer doesn't have to hire him, either.

Many people show up badly in these tests, as noted above. In one sense, this is good news, because the applicant doesn't have to appear perfect, but only not any worse than the others. Of course, the best prospects are for the 25% of the applicants who show up "clean," and this is good reason for trying to "pass" the polygraph.

Some of the methods advised are aimed at suppressing physiological reactions to stress. The simplest is a tranquilizer. One favorite is meprobamate, sold under the trade names of Miltown and Equanil. Actually, almost any sedative will do, even phenobarbital and Dilantin. A subject under "chemical control" will not present the "normal" responses.[11]

A much better and more comprehensive way to suppress stress reactions is by biofeedback.[12] While the original method used for this purpose involved connecting the student to a polygraph so that he could observe the effects of his reactions, today there are many low-cost biofeedback devices available at fairly low cost, and these will serve as well.

Relaxation exercises are the poor man's way to do it, but they can be effective. The techniques are not so well worked out that anyone can do them, but they're fairly simple, and most people find them easy to learn.

Approaching from the other direction is heightening the level of responses to the non-threatening questions used by the examiner for comparison. One way is to use muscular contractions, such as gripping the arms of the chair tightly. This, however, can be visible to an alert polygraph examiner, who will be watching for such behavior anyway. Tightening the toes, sphincter muscles, and biting the tongue are other, less noticeable ways to boost blood pressure and pulse rate. The "thumbtack in the shoe" method is so well-known that it's a legend in its own time.[13]

Controlling physiological responses can go only so far, because many polygraph examiners don't place their entire faith in the charts, although they'll use them as talking points to brow-beat the subject after the test. Many use global scoring, as mentioned above. This is very evident in one text, which devotes more attention to scrutinizing the subject for non-verbal cues than to interpreting the charts.[14]

Anyone seeking to defend himself against polygraph intrusion should be aware that these other factors count for a lot. A testee who is late for the appointment, for example, is considered deceptive. Showing resentment at being required to take the test also counts against the applicant. An applicant who admits to having had a drink or two before coming, or who shows up obviously under the influence, will flunk.[15]

The period right after the test is even more critical in some instances. This is when the examiner asks the subject why he had strong responses to certain questions. He may take the subject through the questions again, to produce another chart. The best reply to probing questions is the simplest one: not to try to explain anything. The subject who keeps his poise and volunteers nothing gives the examiner no opening. If he simply states that he doesn't know why his responses were so strong, and can keep his silence from that point on, he'll do better than one who frantically tries to explain away everything the examiner asks.[16] It's also best for the subject not to ask the examiner if he "passed." Some examiners will, in a last-ditch effort to "break" the subject, hint stongly that he failed. This is a bluff, and the subject should politely excuse himself.

The main point for the examinee to remember is that it's not incumbent on him to explain anything. He should adopt the attitude of "Let the examiner work for his money." A polygraph examination is actually a time and expense saver in pre-employment screening, a quick and dirty substitute for a thorough, and more expensive, background investigation. The candidate should never, not ever, go beyond a simple denial, except perhaps to add "You can check it out. It's true." The employer will not check it out. He doesn't want to spend the bucks.

This point became explosively clear when it turned out that the Chief of Police of a small town was an imposter, having faked his credentials. He had not even graduated from high school, much less seen the police and military service he'd claimed on his application. He'd passed a polygraph examination, and the three police agencies that employed him didn't conduct background investigations to verify the bare facts about his record. Eventually, when some of his officers became involved in arrests that led to huge lawsuits for the town, the council hired a private investigator to do the basic spade-work.

In an informal discussion with the author, this police chief had stated outright that he did not believe in polygraph examinations, and would never ask applicants for his department to submit to one. This was because he knew that it was possible to "beat" the polygraph, having done it himself.

THE VOICE STRESS MACHINES

The doubtful validity of the polygraph is one drawback. Another is that the test is very obvious. It's impossible to test anyone for "truth" without his being aware of it. The secret services of many nations would love to have a method of testing a subject unawares, for obvious reasons, and the American intelligence services sought this sort of device. One result that caught on very quickly after its invention around 1970 was a device to detect changes in the voice produced by stress. The theory is that there's a muscular tremor of about 10 cycles per second in the muscles of the throat and voicebox, during "normal" speech. This tremor disappears under stress. There has been some research into this by scientists not connected with the companies which manufacture these devices, but the results have been inconclusive.[17] There's confirmation of this in a publication by a company that sells polygraphs.[18]

The manufacturers of voice stress machines, their employees, and the users of these devices have claimed astonishingly accurate results.[19] An independent study failed to confirm this level of accuracy, and in fact the polygraph scored better.[20]

Nevertheless, these machines continue to sell, because the promise of covert lie detection is enticing. They supposedly work with any voice sample, such as one taken from a tape recording, obtained through a hidden microphone, and even over the telephone.

These devices, however, offer great potential for harm. Because they're covert, the subject need never know that he's been "tested." This characteristic is extremely attractive to employers seeking methods of pre-employment screening that won't run the risk of lawsuits. The net result is that an applicant can arrive for an interview, unaware that a hidden microphone is picking up his voice for stress testing. Because he's unaware, there's no need to ask him to sign a release, as with the polygraph, and there's no need to coerce him with statements that if he had "nothing to hide, he should not be reluctant to take the test." The applicant can be approved or condemned without ever knowing why.

DRUGS

Popular writers have referred to "truth serum" as the agent used in drug interrogations. This is utterly false. The drugs used are not serums. Furthermore, instead of assuring truth, they release inhibitions and can result in the expression of fantasies.

The Romans coined an expression, *"In vino, veritas"* — "In wine, truth." The effect of alcohol in releasing inhibitions has been known for millenia. People under the influence may become more bold, angry, aggressive, and talkative. It's important to differentiate between truth and release of pent-up emotions. In many instances, the drunk doesn't suddenly pour out all of the important facts of his life. He will weep, laugh, or express anger.

Alcohol also affects judgments. This is well-proven in many areas, such as driving, and performance on the job. In one sense, a person under the influence will tend to be relaxed, less on his guard, and in that sense more prone to make damaging admissions.

Yet, nobody takes seriously the role of alcohol as a "truth drug." While occasionally a police officer or private investigator will supply alcohol to a subject to encourage him to talk, this is a far from infallible method. Obviously no court would allow a witness or suspect to testify while drunk.

There are other drugs which have seen use as "truth drugs."

The barbiturates are sedatives, first invented around the turn of the century in Germany. They were useful for insomnia, and sedation of psychiatric patients. Very recently, they've been used as part of the lethal intravenous "cocktail" given to execute criminals. They're also very effective as anesthetics, and in this application doctors noticed a peculiar effect. Some patients became very talkative during induction, often revealing deeply personal material before falling unconscious.

The Second World War brought a new use for barbiturates. Used as sedatives for "shell-shocked" soldiers, they also found application as a substitute for hypnosis in helping the patients to re-live the frightening experiences that had driven them to their shell-shocked states. The phenomenon was known as "abreaction," and usually produced an immediate relief from symptons.[21] The drug released inhibitions, and allowed the psychiatrist to encourage the patient to discuss his frightening experiences, and to feel again the severe emotions that had been more than his limit, originally. The

111

psychiatrists found that ether was even more effective for this purpose.

A very significant finding was that patients under these drugs became very suggestible, and that they didn't have to re-live the experience which had broken them down. The psychiatrist could suggest an imaginary situation, and the patients would accept it, and show terror as if they were re-living something that had actually happened.22 The strong emotions would produce a state of "transmarginal inhibition" which would eliminate the symptoms.

Police had been experimenting with "truth drugs" for some years, and having mixed results. Some claimed that having a psychiatrist inject suspects with barbital produced amazing confessions. Others had indifferent results. Gradually, it became clear that some subjects might confess, their inhibitions having been suppressed by the drug, but others fantasized, prompted by suggestions from the interrogator.

There have been experiments with scopolamine, an alkaloid derived from plants. This produces a state of mental confusion, and amnesia. Combined with a barbiturate, it produces "twilight sleep," a light anesthesia which results in the patient's not remembering the events. There's an obvious advantage to a drug which wipes out the subject's memory of having been drugged. The possibilites of covert and extra-legal interrogations are many, but the drugs simply don't work as expected. The combination of mental confusion and heightened suggestibility made hash out of interrogations.

The amphetamines provided another opportunity for chemical confession-seeking. A dose of benzedrine or dexedrine produces a feeling of well-being and confidence, and this supposedly provokes

112

uninhibited replies to an interrogator's questions. A very powerful variant, methedrine, was used in some instances.

One subject gave this account of his interrogation: "I was taken to a room with a couch, and told to lie down. The psychiatrist injected a drug into the vein of my arm. He told me that it was Pervitin, which I found out later was methedrine. He turned on a tape recorder while he was waiting for the drug to act. I felt a sort of rush, but a mild one. I felt very good, alert, and more alive than usually. I'd been told that this drug would make me tell the truth, but felt that I could lie if I wished, anyway. The doctor asked me a series of questions, which I answered truthfully. This session went on for over an hour, with him asking me the questions again and again. Finally, he turned the tape machine off, and told his nurse to give me a couple of phenobarbital pills to counter the Pervitin's effects. I could tell that he was unhappy, because I hadn't given him the answers he wanted, but what the hell, I was innocent anyway!" 23

This illustrates one of the remarkable features of technological methods of interrogation. The practitioners seem to have an absolute faith in their techniques, and are at a loss to explain it away when there's a failure.

EXOTIC DRUGS

During WWII, the Office of Strategic Services issued "truth pills," containing the active ingredient of marijuana, to their agents. Supposedly, one of these pills would compel the subject to tell the truth. Administering the drug was allegedly just a matter of dissolving it in the subject's drink.

Apparently these pills weren't very effective, because once the CIA was established after the war, the search for a good truth drug resumed. Partly because of the delusion that the Soviets already had such mind-bending drugs, American researchers made strong efforts to find free-world counterparts.

A Swiss pharmacologist named Hoffman had discovered the effects of Lysergic Acid in 1943. This drug has psychotropic effects somewhat like the naturally occurring drug mescaline, which has been known to American Indians for centuries. The CIA and the U.S. Army decided to explore the properties of this drug as an interrogation aid. In so doing, they made use of unwilling subjects for their experiments.[24]

Using people for medical experiments without their consent is a violation of both law and medical ethics. This is especially true if the experiments result in harm to the subjects. This is the sort of experimentation that led to some of the War Crimes Trials of German doctors after the Allied victory. Nevertheless, the CIA was able to employ American doctors to conduct experiments with drugs that proved fatal for their subjects.

One such was a man who was a patient in a psychiatric hospital. He was administered LSD without being told what the drug was nor what its effects would be. He went into a coma and died. Another, a CIA employee, was dosed with LSD at a party. He was so severely affected by the drug that he jumped out of a hotel window and died from the fall.

There were many other instances of CIA experimentation on American citizens who were guilty of no crimes, in efforts to develop ways of manipulating peoples' minds. Some experiments with massive doses of electro-shock treatment were tried, in an effort to produce a lasting amnesia and total submergence of the personality. Various forms

114

of "psychosurgery" were financed by the CIA towards the same ends.

Electro-shock "therapy" had seen wide use before becoming largely discredited. It had been used for punishment as well, a control measure to enforce obedience in psychiatric patients. Interrogators also experimented with it as a means of breaking down subjects' resistance to questioning. It had been noticed by psychiatrists that the patients' personalities gradually disintegrated under repeated electro-shocks. Logically, the will to resist should also disappear. It did, but with this came other effects; confusion and amnesia. Interrogators found that it was futile to interrogate subjects whose memories had been wiped out. The amnesia was usually temporary, but a prolonged series of "treatments" had a more severe effect, resulting in permanent memory loss.

In many instances, the subjects were psychiatric patients. It became very convenient to experiment on these patients, for an obvious reason: if they complained, or revealed what had been done to them, their testimony could easily be discredited. Using mental patients also allows careful selection to avoid embarrassing problems with relatives. Some chronic patients confined in long-term wards at state hospitals have been abandoned by their relatives. They never get visits and nobody in the outside world takes an interest in their welfare. Without visiting relatives to monitor their condition, these patients can be subjected to almost any sort of "treatment" desired.

ADDING IT UP

Technological means of interrogation have proved disappointing. The slick gadgets have not lived up to the promises of their promoters. Part of the reason is their primitive state of development. Another is that "truth" and "lie" are not as simple concepts as they first appear, and the ways in which people react to them are so varied that detecting deception is extraordinarily difficult at best.

Chemical highs to produce a euphoric, uninhibited state can easily result in confessions that aren't worth the paper on which they're written. The huge amount of research has so far produced disappointing results. Congressional investigations have uncovered bureaucratic boondoggles, but little in concrete accomplishments. The search for an electronic or chemical truth-producer is still unfulfilled.

Sources

1. *A Tremor in the Blood,* David Thoreson Lykken, New York, McGraw-Hill, 1981, p. 50.

2. *Ibid.,* p. 30.

3. *Ibid.,* pp. 55-62. Also relevant are the findings of the Office of Technology Assessment of the United States Congress, November, 1983. This study, *Scientific Validity of Polygraph Testing,* is a survey of the relevant research by psychologists, psychiatrists, jurists, and law enforcement officials. The general conclusions were that while there is some evidence to support the validity of the polygraph in criminal investigations, there's little or no evidence to show that it's valid in other applications. These include pre-employment screening. There's also evidence to show that various types of countermeasures work, the simplest and best overall being drugs.

4. Discussions with polygraph examiners and the author. It might be optimistic to expect that these people would willingly admit something which would directly threaten their livelihoods. Polygraph examiners tend to dismiss objections with the dogmatic statement: "It works! I've seen it work!", or something similar.

5. *Telling Lies,* Paul Ekman, New York, W.W. Norton & Company, 1985, pp. 65-79.

6. *Tremor in the Blood,* pp. 205-215.

7. *Passing the Pre-Employment Lie Detector Test,* Robert Duggar, Jasper, Alabama, 1984, pp. 6-10.

8. Related to the author by an applicant to a police agency. This man was asked if he'd masturbated as an adolescent, had sexual relations with members of the same sex, or animals, and a number of other questions regarding his sexual life.

9. *Tremor in the Blood,* p. 238.

10. Passing the Pre-Employment Lie Detector Test, pp. 4-5.

11. Related to the author by a polygraph examiner.

12. *Tremor in the Blood,* p. 238.

13. *Ibid.,* pp. 238-239.

14. *Advanced Lie Detection Techniques,* Ralph D. Thomas, Austin, Texas, Thomas Publications, 1985.

This text advises examiners to watch for gestures, twitching, perspiration, crossing of legs, and other physical signs that supposedly indicate deception.

15. *Passing the Pre-Employment Lie Detector Test,* pp. 19-20.

16. *Ibid.,* pp. 31-32.

17. *Tremor in the Blood,* pp. 154-155.

18. *Lie Detection Manual,* Dr. Harold Feldman, Belleville, New Jersey, Law Enforcement Associates, 1982, p. 17.

19. *Tremor in the Blood,* pp. 156-157.

20. *Ibid.,* pp. 157-158.

21. *Battle for the Mind,* William Sargant, Garden City, New York, 1957, pp. 65-67.

22. *Ibid.,* pp. 72-73.

23. Related to the author by the subject.

24. *Behavior Modification,* Richard Camellion, Boulder, Colorado, Paladin Press, 1978, pp. 71-84.

TORTURE

In certain countries where American Constitutional protections don't apply, there has been extensive use of physical torture. There's also been torture in the United States, although perhaps not as commonly as in some other countries.

Torture during interrogation has existed for so long that it's become institutionalized. Evidence of this institutionalization is its emergence into slang. The expression, "the third degree," is mainly American. Reportedly, it means a rigorous experience, comparable to the treatment that Freemasons allegedly get when they pass into their "Third Degree."

The corresponding expression in French is "passage au tabac," which translates loosely as "the tobacco treatment." The connection between rigorous interrogation and tobacco is hard to understand, but slang isn't always logical. The French "Police Judiciaire," the criminal detective force, has a reputation for tough methods in solving crimes.

The rationale behind torture is very simple, but the Twentieth Century has brought certain complications, mainly in the way we think about it. The main fact is that torture is a way of coercing information from the subject. It's an attitude changing technique that converts a subject from tight-lipped negativism to willing verbosity.

There are several objections to the use of torture, and we'd better deal with them before getting into the nuts and bolts of the methods. Some objections are practical. Let's deal with them first.

1. Torture's usually illegal. The Geneva Convention forbids its use on prisoners of war. The laws of all our states and the Fifth Amendment to the Constitution make it clear that a confession extracted through physical torture is illegal and inadmissible. The police officer is open to prosecution if he uses physical torture. This is a strong deterrent, no matter how eager an officer may be to "make" his case. Sacrificing a career for the sake of a quick confession usually isn't worth it.

2. Torture often leaves marks, which makes it difficult to conceal or deny. A court will easily accept a defendant's claim of torture if he's covered with cuts and bruises, unless the officer can produce a convincing alternative explanation. Saying that the prisoner "fell down the stairs" no longer serves as an adequate explanation. "Resisting arrest" requires corroboration, to be on the safe side.

3. Torturing a subject simply induces him to say what the interrogator wants to hear, to stop the pain. Therefore, any confession so obtained is invalid.

This is true when the officer uses torture to obtain a simple confession, but if he's seeking information another set of rules applies. When interrogating to obtain leads, officers find that subjects lie without being tortured, too. Pain or lack of pain have little to do with the reliability of the information extracted, only the quantity. The interrogator has to use controls to ensure that the subject's providing the correct information. This applies whether he uses torture or not.

120

4. There's an additional hazard in areas where torture isn't standard practice. The passive compliance of fellow officers, who may be witnesses to the torture, isn't certain. This is especially true today, when higher standards are coming to police work, and the torturer is looked upon as a brute. Police administrators are encouraging whistle-blowing, and the code of silence that's been traditional with the police "brotherhood" is weaker than it's ever been.

The intangible objections to torture are:

1. Torture is uncivilized behavior, not worthy of a police officer who's sworn to uphold the laws. This is a value judgment, and anyone contemplating the use of torture must first ask himself if he considers his subject "civilized." A terrorist, mass murderer, or similar type isn't the best sort of human being, and the officer may feel that his prisoner doesn't deserve any consideration.

Another relevant factor is that, while the use of torture by civil police is probably declining, security police officers feel that a higher purpose justifies torture. Defending the security of the state is a higher purpose, and sterner measures are allowed. This is why, for example, security agencies tend to use routinely illegal methods that are denied to the regular police, such as wiretapping and entrapment.

2. Torture dishonors and degrades the one who uses or condones it, and makes him no better than his enemy. This may be true, in the eyes of many people, but the decision can't hang on this alone. The officer contemplating torture must also consider what purpose it will serve. Certain extreme circumstances place the investigating officer in a dilemma.

One such situation is the capture of a terrorist. Trying to persuade the terrorist to reveal the location of the other members of his group is important because their apprehension will usually save the lives of innocent people whom they would kill if left free. It's easy to turn one's nose up at such a situation and walk away from it, saying that torture would be self-degrading, but the officer who makes this decision is passively allowing innocent people to be killed.

More common examples are those of recidivist criminals who have never been convicted. A key witness always "disappears" or suffers a "loss of memory" before the trial. Vital evidence vanishes from the property room. The investigating officer does a slow burn while the arrestee sneeringly answers that he does know his rights and that he wants a lawyer. This can tempt an officer to try severe methods.

THE LIMITS OF TORTURE

Experienced police officers know that there are practical limits to torture. These limits lessen the effectiveness of torture and reduce the number of instances in which torture can be useful.

1. In many cases, the torture must leave no marks because it's later necessary to release the subject or to present him in court. This confines the officer to methods that don't mutilate. Modern technology provides enough methods for applying pressure without leaving marks, and the officer must choose carefully.

2. The subject's endurance may be a factor. There have been instances of subjects dying under forced interrogation. In some instances, the subject's

health is frail, and he dies from shock or a heart attack. In other instances, the subject is so stubborn and resistant that he dies from exhaustion, without talking. Jean Moulin, the French Maquis leader, was one such, who valued the safety of his comrades more than he did his own life.

It's vital for the officer to understand that the physical weakening he inflicts upon his subject can also be life-threatening, and to take precautions. It's desirable to have a medical examination before severe interrogation, and to balance carefully the measures used against the subject's health. As a practical matter, in some instances it's not necessary for the prisoner to survive interrogation, and the only requirement is that he provide useful information before he expires.

3. Time can be a severe limitation. It may be necessary to "break" a subject before a certain event happens. In some instances, it's possible to detain a subject for only a limited time without further evidence. If detention depends on information and leads obtainable only from the subject, the officer's at a severe disadvantage.

In other instances, it may be necessary to obtain the location of co-conspirators from the subject before they can be warned and escape. This makes the interrogation urgent.

In rare instances, lives may depend on obtaining information from a subject. A terrorist may know the location of a time bomb, and extracting this information from him will save lives. Other information may also be vital. If it's possible to obtain the identity of the target of an assassination attempt before it takes place, extra security precautions may avert the killing.

It's easy to see that torture, physical or mental, is neither an overwhelming evil nor a cure-all. It has its pros and cons, and there are severe practical limitations to its use.

A QUICK HISTORY OF TORTURE

We're going to skip lightly over the many elaborate devices used in man's history of inflicting pain upon his fellow man. Most of the mechanical contrivances were technically very inefficient, and made up more as works of art than as technical aids. As works of art, they're evidence of the sick minds that devised them.

Torture in ancient times was understandably crude by today's standards. Kicks and punches predominated, with an occasional technical artifact. The Middle Ages saw the refinement of torture into almost an art form. Medieval interrogators used elaborate devices such as the rack and the "iron maiden" to inflict pain on their unfortunate subjects. The most peculiar aspect of the interrogators working for the Inquisition was their self-righteous belief that they were torturing their subjects for their own good. At the time, the prevailing belief was that apostasy was the road to hell. Bringing a person back onto the right track, the "correct" religion, would save his soul. It was therefore legitimate to use torture to save a person's soul. Saving the subject from eternal damnation was the main purpose, even if it meant torturing and killing him.

The rack was a mechanical device to stretch the spinal column, inflicting severe pain. The interrogator tied the victim to the rack, using ropes to attach his arms to one rack and his feet to the other. A pinion, turned with a lever, moved the two racks apart, applying stretch to the body.

The iron maiden was a coffin-shaped container, with spikes inside. Anyone shut into this device would find his body pierced by the spikes. Depending on the length of the spikes, and the individual's resistance, the experience could easily be lethal.

The strappado is a simple technique requiring only an overhead beam or pulley and some rope. A rope, running from the subject's hands tied behind his back, runs up and over a beam or pulley. Pulling on the free end of the rope brings the subject's hands and arms up backward, and will eventually dislocate the shoulders. It's not necessary to go this far to cause extreme pain.

Other tortures used during the early times were various forms of heat. Holding someone's limbs in a fire would be persuasive, as would touching his body with hot irons. Inserting red-hot irons into body orifices was used for torture and as a method of execution.

PRACTICAL TORTURE TODAY

Some of the methods are very simple, consisting of kicks and punches, while others run the gamut from mechanical devices up to electric shock machines applied to the genitals and other sensitive parts of the body. Torture exists today, and it exists in this country. Recently, two New York City police officers were convicted of using a stun gun to coerce information from a suspect.[1] This is only one incident, but it's one that not only came to the surface, but resulted in a trial and conviction. Because for every conviction there are many more that go free, it's obvious that even today there are many instances of torture practiced by the police.

The main point to decide before using torture is whether the subject must survive the experience. If he must live to stand trial, it's necessary to be careful not to leave signs of torture. This precludes any especially rigorous measures such as bone-breaking or other mutilations. If the setting is a guerrilla war, for example, and there's been extreme brutality on both sides, anything goes.

The secondary point is that the subject must live long enough to yield information.2 Even when "anything goes," it's counter-productive to kill the subject before he has a chance to talk. This is why the usual plan is graduated torture, which becomes more severe as the interrogation continues.

SELECTING THE TORTURER

Who applies physical severities depends on the nature of the police organization. In many instances, especially in the West, the arresting officer is also the interrogator. In one sense, this promotes amateurism. In another, there's no opportunity to develop professional interrogators. This can be both good and bad.

Training and developing a corps of professional interrogators can be beneficial, because it concentrates the pool of skill. In fact, some countries have training establishments for interrogators. During the Algerian crisis, French security forces schooled their interrogators at the "St. Joan of Arc Interrogation School." The curriculum included use of the Gestapo electric-shock device. In Portugal, interrogators have attended classroom sessions, learning by films and tapes the arcane techniques of physical interrogation. In Uruguay, aspiring secret policemen attended lab sessions where instructors demonstrated torture techniques on human subjects.3

This can become bizarre. The Greek secret police set up a training camp for novice interrogators, and the training methods in this school were designed to brutalize the interrogators by inflicting brutalities upon them. They were beaten by their instructors and comrades to desensitize them to normal human values.4

An additional danger in selecting professional interrogators is that of being infiltrated by people who are not only happy in their works, but who like it too much. Police work has an appeal to coercive people, and a job as interrogator in a setting where torture is allowed is irresistable to a professional sadist. This is what explains the interrogator who is disappointed when his subject "cracks" too quickly. This also explains the more bizarre personalities, such as the Chilean interrogator who directed sessions that concentrated on sexual torture.5 Another Chiean interrogator was an air force officer, TDY'd to the secret police, who tortured children in front of their parents to induce confessions.6

Staffers such as these are more interested in the ride than the destination, and are not the best people for obtaining results. It's important for a case officer or supervisor to monitor the work of a professional interrogator carefully, to ensure that he keeps his priorities straight. The supervisor should not be surprised at anything. If he observes signs of sexual excitement in the interrogator, he should immediately relieve him of his duties and appoint another who can keep a better perspective.

THE METHODS

This discussion will center upon simple and practical methods that don't require elaborate, hard to obtain, or hard to construct equipment. Experience has shown that simple techniques are best because they work as effectively and cause as much pain, and are easier to apply. All of the technical aids mentioned herein are commonly available through regular sources of supply or are easy to improvise. Some, such as handcuffs, are standard police equipment. Other items, such as matches and butane lighters, can be found in almost any desk drawer. Special equipment such as X-acto hobby knives, stun guns, needles, and syringes, aren't costly and some can even be bought in a supermarket.

Some interrogators feel that fear and anticipation are the keys to success, and that it's helpful to make clear to the subject that he's going to be in "a world of hurt," before actually starting the torture. In some extreme instances, interrogators have had their prisoners walk by torture chambers from which they could hear the cries of the unfortunates. In other cases, tape recordings of anguished screams have been played outside the interrogation room to "soften up" the subject psychologically.

The interrogator can structure the session to build anticipation. Before applying a new method, he should explain to the subject exactly what he's going to do, leaving no details to the imagination. If he's about to insert a needle, he should mention it if the needle's not sterile. If he's about to burn the fingertips with a butane lighter, mentioning that butane burns at well over 1000 degrees can help induce fear.

A basic principle of torture is that the process starts with relatively mild methods and escalates to severe ones if the subject resists. In some subjects, prolonged torture can build resistance, and it's best to exhaust the milder methods first. Another reason is that prolonged severities can literally drive a subject out of his mind, and it's much more difficult to elicit cooperation from a psychotic subject.

Inducing Fatigue

This is a well-known secret police method, but what's not as well-publicized is its widespread ease of application in regular police interrogations. Civil liberties lawyers are familiar with this method because it's so commonly used.

The simplest technique for inducing fatigue is to keep the subject awake by endless interrogation. Teams of interrogators switch off, asking the same questions repeatedly, to keep the subject from nodding off. Civil libertarians object to marathon interrogation sessions, a fact which the investigating officer must keep in mind.

Another way is forced exercise. The simplest way is to keep the subject standing, with only a guard to watch him. Another is to keep the subject kneeling. This technique can also cause pain, if the subject kneels on a broomstick or piece of dowel.

Exertion speeds up fatigue. Running in place, sit-ups, push-ups, or simple marching will burn calories and induce fatigue.7 During all of this, withholding food and water will bring the subject closer to physical collapse. It's important to monitor the subject carefully, though, as severe collapse from heat stroke or a heart attack can be counter-productive.

Although a guard is usually sufficient to monitor and control the subject during this period, it can be productive for the interrogator to pop in occasionally to ask the subject if he's willing to cooperate. This provides opportunity to induce anticipation by brief mention of what's in store for him later, and to reinforce the idea that he's completely in the interrogator's power.

Starvation and Thirst

Depriving the subject of food and water causes extreme discomfort and often lessens resistance. The investigating officer will have to judge carefully whether the effect upon the prisoner's health is too severe, and therefore counter-productive. A comatose subject can't divulge much information.

Restricting Breathing

Drowning is an old method of causing extreme distress. With a young and healthy subject, it can work. A debilitated subject can go into shock.

There are several ways of cutting off the air supply. Simple choking works, but leaves marks. A plastic bag over the head also stops breathing. A large and heavy wet rag over the face will impede breathing enough to be very uncomfortable. Dunking the head also works.

These techniques can combine with psychologically-oriented methods to enhance the effect. Dunking the head has an additional measure of discomfort if the prisoner's head goes into an unflushed toilet. Similarly, the wet rag can be wet with urine. Forcing a smaller urine-soaked rag into the subject's mouth can induce gagging. The officer must be watchful that the subject doesn't asphyxiate in his own vomit.

Restraint

Restraint of some sort is also useful as a preliminary, "softening-up" method before the start of a formal session of interrogation.

Every police officer knows that handcuffs can be very uncomfortable, if worn for hours. If closed tightly, they can be painful very quickly, because they

cut off circulation and press on muscles, bones, cartilage, and nerves. A pair of tight handcuffs will quickly cause the hands to swell, which increases the pain, and can cause gangrene if too extreme.

Another way to "soften up" a prisoner is to tie his arms behind his back. Restrained this way, he can be left in a cell for hours or days. Tying him to a hard chair is even more uncomfortable, and is painful if he's restrained so tightly that he can't shift his weight.

Tying him down to a sturdy table offers more possibilities. The table can be improvised, but it must be sturdy enough to hold up against any struggle the subject may make. A quick improvisation is to tie the prisoner down with ropes passing around the table. A more sophisticated method is to have metal loops through which to thread the ropes or cuffs. Using hand and leg cuffs permits fastening the subject down very quickly.

If a packing crate large enough to hold the subject is available, confining him in it for hours or days will soften him up. The main requirement is that it must be small enough to keep him from stretching out or even moving very much. Keeping him doubled up in a crate no larger than 3 feet cubed is effective. It may be desirable to nail him in, but rope or a latch are quicker to release. Spraying tear gas into the container from time to time will increase the subject's discomfort.

A bonus effect comes if time permits. Inevitably, the prisoner will have to perform natural bodily functions. Keeping him confined results in his soiling himself with urine and/or feces. This isn't physically painful, but can be psychologically degrading, especially if he's dressed in his own clothing rather than a prison uniform.

Some methods of restraint are designed to be painful in themselves. Tying the fingers with a piece of dowel or a pencil between them is painful. A Kubotan or similar police defensive device is a commonly-available tool for this purpose.

Restraint is also necessary during the more rigorous phases of interrogation. This is why an investment in a sturdy table with the necessary accessories is wise if physical interrogation is regular practice. Some of the more forceful methods, such as a shock from a stun gun, will cause an unrestrained subject to hit the ceiling.

Other choices for restraint are a sturdy chair and a ladder. The ladder's an especially good improvisation because it allows quick access to both front and back.8 The rungs are convenient points for fastening handcuffs.

Pressure Points, Twists, and Locks

These are simple methods, not requiring instruments, which can cause severe pain, without leaving marks if skillfully done. The advantage is that these are excellent field expedient techniques which an interrogator can apply with minimal preparation.

A key-chain Kubotan.

Pressing a finger upward where the jaw meets the neck will cause excruciating pain with only a few pounds' pressure. Some advise using a Kubotan or other instrument for this, but it's really not necessary. A finger is enough.

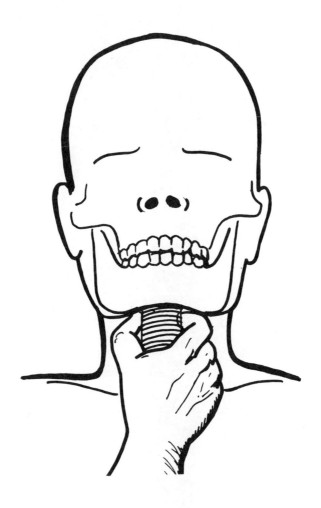

Pressing the thumb and forefinger into the throat and making them meet behind the windpipe causes severe pain, but without danger of strangulation. Although it's possible also to crush the windpipe, severe pain occurs long before this happens.

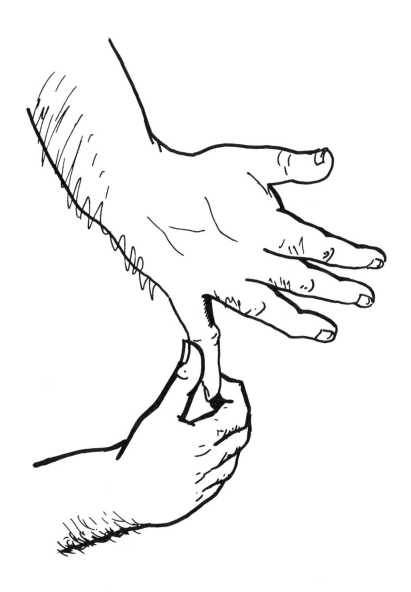

Bending fingers backward causes pain, and is also
an easy way to break them. Pulling them apart also
causes pain and can tear ligaments and muscles.
The same applies to the toes.

Applying pressure against the elbow, against the movement of the joint, will cause pain. It's also very easy to break the elbow by this maneuver.

Applying certain wrestling holds can cause pain. An arm-lock, hammer-lock, or leg-lock causes pain with less risk of permanent damage than pressure against the elbow or knee.

Blows

These can be with the open hand, as with slaps, the fist, or with a mechanical aid, such as a stick or whip. Anyone who uses blows must be discreet, because it's important not to knock the subject unconscious or to inflict a lethal blow.

A slap to the face is the hardest blow that should fall upon the head. The interrogator should avoid even this if he's unusually muscular or tends to get carried away. A brain concussion won't help the situation. Using both hands to slap the ears simultaneously can cause great pain because of pressure on the eardrums, but it also risks breaking the eardrums. This can be undesirable. Such a blow can deafen, incapacitate, and even cause total unconsciousness.

Blows to the solar plexus are very painful, but can be life-threatening. A severe punch can cause the subject to spew his last meal over the officer's uniform, and also rupture the liver and spleen. An internal hemorrhage can kill the subject before the officer's aware that anything's seriously wrong.

Blows to the genitals cause pain, but here the danger is causing unconsciousness. A punch or kick to the testicles can cause permanent damage, something to consider if the subject must eventually appear in court

Blows using a stick, rubber hose, wet towel, or other mechanical aid should avoid bony parts of the body unless the intent is to break bones. Generally, a mild blow on unprotected skin will cause pain with less chance of severe injury than a hard blow on a clothed body. This is one reason for stripping the subject naked before commencing the interrogation. The psychological reason for nakedness is covered in the appropriate chapter.

Some interrogators feel that breaking the fingers is desirable, because breaking these bones is not life-threatening. This is more effective if the subject works in an occupation in which use of the hands is important. A typist, surgeon, or pianist is vulnerable to this tactic, and damage is psychologically devastating. In practice, a blow is not the best way to break fingers, because the impact often deadens the nerves and reduces the pain. Crushing with pliers is more prolonged and more painful, and can be more effective. The toes are equally vulnerable to simple breaking or crushing.

Friction

Using sandpaper or similarly abrasive materials and instruments can traumatize large areas of skin without threatening the subject's life. Rubbing the skin until it bleeds causes the maximum pain by this method.

Crushing

Although exotic crushing devices litter the history of torture, their elaborate nature was merely a concession to the sick minds of their builders. For simple, utilitarian infliction of pain, simple and commonly-available devices are suitable.

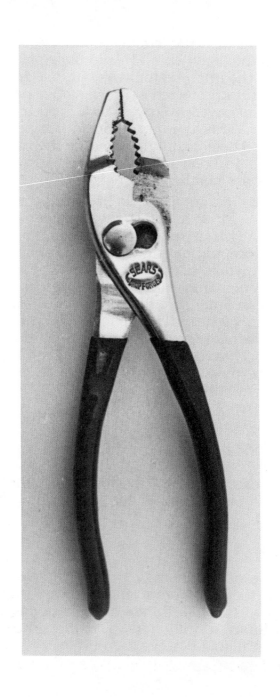

140

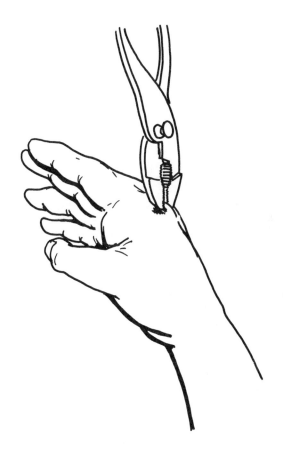

A pair of pliers is simplest. This allows applying pain to almost any part of the body where soft tissue is available to nip between the jaws. The main advantage of pliers is the margin of safety built in. It's almost impossible to kill someone inadvertently with pliers, although the pain can be severe enough to cause fainting. Using pliers can easily leave marks, though. Crushing an eyelid or ripping it off leaves unmistakable evidence of torture. Crushing patches of skin leaves severe contusions and hematomas which can take weeks or months to heal. Pliers are also useful for extracting fingernails or teeth.

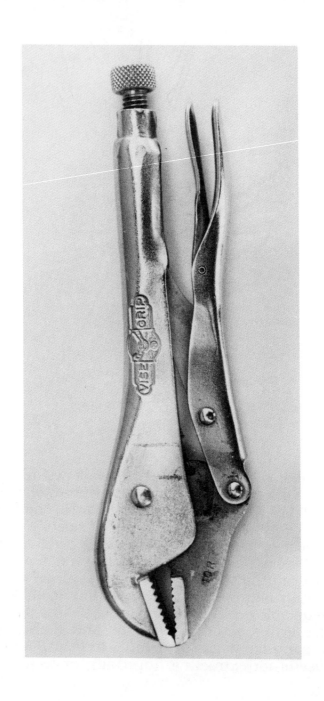

142

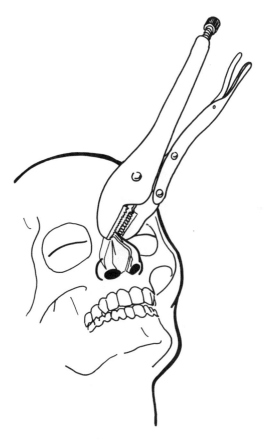

One step up the scale is the vise-grip, a plier with compound leverage which can crush a bone. This is useful for crushing fingers and toes. Applied to the bridge of the nose, it will crush the bone there. Twisting the vise-grip while squeezing the bridge of the nose can cause severe pain.

Caution: The vise-grip develops much more pressure than necessary for use on soft tissue. While it can serve to rip off patches of skin and produce mutilating injuries, the extreme pressure can also crush nerves and thereby deaden the pain. This is why use on the breasts or genitals is not advisable.

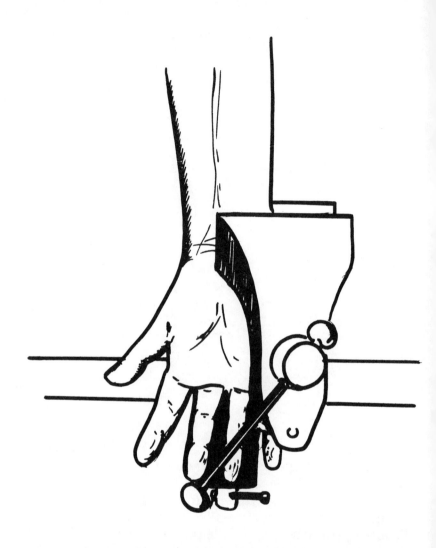

The machinist's bench vise is the top of the line in hand tools. It develops enough pressure to crush bones. The larger bench vises, with jaws four inches or more in width, will allow insertion of a wrist or ankle. Because these joints have several bones, they're easily damaged by moderate pressure in a vise.

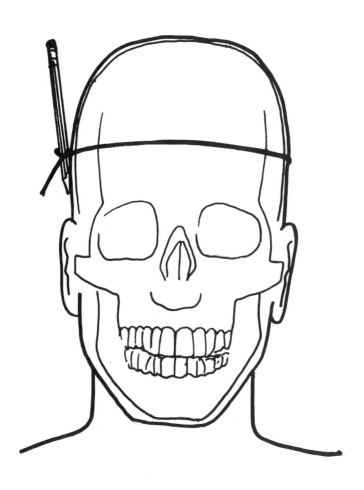

The tourniquet is easy to improvise and can be extremely painful. The flexible band can be string, rope, or wire, and the dowel to tighten it can be a pencil, piece of rebar, broomstick, etc.9

It's possible to use a tourniquet on almost any part of the body. The limbs are obvious targets. Wrapping the constricting band around the head can be very painful, causing a severe headache that lasts long after release of the pressure. The neck, however, is not a target because a tourniquet will cut off the blood flow to the brain and cause unconsciousness before the subject experiences much pain.

The tourniquet can be very effective against the male genitals. Tying off the scrotum especially can be painful. The advantage is that, because of their sensitivity to pain, the testicles require very little pressure. This lessens the chances of causing permanent injury.

One feature of the tourniquet is that most people know that a tourniquet left in place for more than a few minutes can cause death of the tissue and gangrene as a consequence of cutting off the blood supply. The interrogator can bring this out to anyone who seems unaware of it. This provides the psychological pressure of impending mutilation.

Cold

The use of cold can be very effective with some people, but it has two severe drawbacks. One is that cold numbs the senses, and this makes it ineffective after a few minutes. The other is that it can be life-threatening. Hypothermia can kill, and even the momentary shock of being plunged into a bath of ice water can stop the heart in some apparently healthy subjects.

Keeping a person in a cold room, therefore, is counter-productive, unless it's just cold enough to induce discomfort and keep him shivering. The ice bath, on the other hand, is momentary, but if the subject survives the first dousing, he can be plunged in repeatedly.10 It's hard for anyone who hasn't taken a plunge into ice water to realize that it's actually painful, and that the threat of being warmed up, dressed in dry clothing, only to be dunked again can be a powerful inducement to cooperate.

Heat

Using heat to induce cooperation is an old technique, but it requires careful management. Experience has shown that local application of intense heat is quicker and more effective than exposing the whole body to moderate heat. Some ancient torturers used to leave their victims tied up in the hot sun for hours or days, but this is slow and carries with it the dangers of dehydration and heat stroke.

To understand the reasoning behind using heat to induce compliance, we must touch lightly upon burns as injuries. First-degree burns are painful, heal quickly, and usually don't leave scars. Second-degree burns destroy the deeper skin layers and leave some scars. The problem for the interrogator is that the deeper skin layers contain the pain receptors. Third-degree burns destroy the skin completely, exposing the underlying tissue. Although the skin's pain receptors are destroyed, a third-degree burn is very painful because the nerve endings of the underlying organs are now exposed. Unfortunately, third-degree burns are life-threatening, unless they involve only a very small area.

There's another type of burn, usually mentioned only in emergency rooms: the fourth-degree burn. This involves charring the underlying muscles, connective tissue, and bone. It can happen from prolonged and severe heat, such as a torch applied to the tissue. Although the history of torture contains examples of inducing fourth-degree burns, this is overkill.

The main point about burns for the interrogator is that the amount of skin burned is what determines if the burn is life-threatening. Charring a fingertip can be very painful, but not a deadly threat. A severe sunburn covering the entire body is more dangerous.

Burning selected parts of the body with various simple devices is the best method. The crudest and least expensive way is a match. Using a phosphorous match has one advantage over the other methods. The phosphorus produces a deep burn with severe lingering pain which is more severe than the after-pain of a burn from a lighter or a soldering iron.

A cigarette is next. This produces controlled heat, and the interrogator can prolong the agony by first holding it close to the skin, then closer, to increase the severity of the burn. The limitation of a cigarette is that it can't be used to reach deep areas, as pressure on the tip puts it out.

A butane lighter gives a quick and controllable flame. Most models of disposable lighters (the Scripto is a good example) have flame adjustments for this purpose. With an adjustable flame it's possible to attain a more subtle effect. Burning the pubic hair before attacking the genitals builds anticipation with less risk of sending the subject into shock.

The soldering iron is almost ideal, but it requires a plug-in power source. If the interrogation is conducted indoors, as most are, this isn't a problem, but a literal "field interrogation," as with prisoners of war, precludes the use of a soldering iron.

One way to build anticipation with the soldering iron is to insert it into a body orifice, such as the ear, nose, or anus, and then plug it in. The controllability of the soldering iron permits applying pain with minimal tissue damage.

This is important. The problem with burning is that it also destroys nerve endings, as we've covered, and this somewhat mitigates the pain. Hospital employees assigned to burn wards know that the pain of a severe burn is unbearable, and so severe that drugs aren't fully effective in controlling it. This isn't helpful in interrogation. Severe burns are life-threatening. They're also permanently disfiguring, which can be important if the subject is allowed to survive the interrogation.

Sharp Instruments

Simple tools such as pins, needles, nails, and hobby knives are all that's necessary to inflict enough pain for interrogation.

Inserting pins or nails under the fingernails and toenails is one way to inflict pain. Another way is to simply jab at other sensitive areas of the body. It's not necessary to concentrate on the eyes and genitals, as the skin in the armpit and inner thigh is very tender.

A fine point about inserting needles is that a quick jab is painful, but it's only a sting. Inserting the needle slowly and leaving it in is far more painful.

Pictured below is a hobby knife.

Needles also offer opportunities for credible threats that may work without having to implement them. The interrogator, after pricking the subject several times, can threaten to insert a needle into an eyeball. If the anxiety build-up's been adequate, this can elicit compliance.

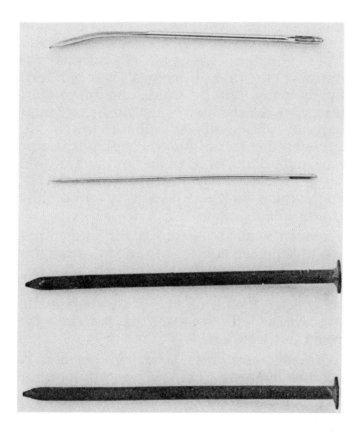

A hobby knife's useful, if one's conveniently available. Inserting the point under fingernails causes pain, as does making small cuts in selected areas of the body. If used on the ear, it's important to avoid excess enthusiasm which might lead to puncturing the eardrum, as interrupting communication with the subject would impede the interrogation.

Chemicals and Drugs

This section will cover only commonplace chemicals, not psychological drugs, which belong in another chapter. The use of various noxious chemicals can aid interrogation, not only by inducing pain, but by producing discomfort and humiliation. An example is a strong laxative, such as castor oil, olive oil, or others which can be administered surreptitiously. Phenolphthalein is the active ingredient in Ex-Lax and other over-the-counter laxatives. It's a white, tasteless, odorless powder, which makes it possible to conceal in both food and hot drinks.

A laxative's most useful for softening up. If the plan's to keep the subject confined or restrained, so that he can't attend to his toilet needs, he'll soil himself quickly and uncontrollably when the laxative takes effect. A couple of days of this treatment is all that's worthwhile because his bowels will have emptied out by then.

Commonly available scouring powder causes severe and enduring pain when sprinkled into the eyes. This is more intense if it's chlorinated powder. There's a severe risk of causing blindness with this treatment.

Chlorinated liquid bleach causes retching, gagging, coughing, and nausea when poured down the throat. If the subject's uncooperative and won't open his mouth, it's necessary to risk injury to the fingers by trying to pry his mouth open. A rubber baby enema syringe can be used to squirt the bleach into his nostrils, where it will cause instant irritation and the excess will trickle down his throat.

Surprisingly, carbonated beverages are also useful for this technique.11 Using Seven-Up eliminates the risk of permanent injury.

A quick and dirty improvisation is to urinate into the subject's mouth if it's open, and into the nostrils if he keeps his mouth shut. Despite the recent proliferation of females in police work, this technique is best left to male interrogators because only males can aim the stream of urine with enough precision.

A can of Mace or other tear gas spray is usually available. This will irritate not only delicate respiratory passages, but skin on various parts of the body. Spraying the crotch area usually makes the subject extremely uncomfortable. Caution: do not spray directly into the eyes unless the risk of causing blindness is unimportant.

Acid causes irritation and pain when in contact with tissue. Strong acids, such as battery acid, will burn the nasal passages, but using too much risks causing death. Vinegar, which contains dilute acetic acid and has an overpowering odor, is equally effective when squirted into the nostrils, and much safer. Injecting acid under the skin is also painful, and can cause large bleeding ulcers to develop after a few hours. These will heal very slowly and can be disfiguring.

Using a syringe to introduce various substances into the body can cause effects far out of proportion to the sting of the needle. One technique is to inject

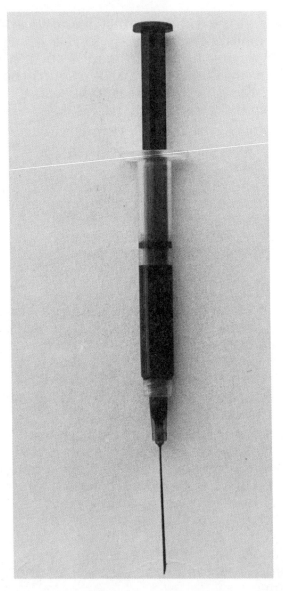

This syringe contains stamp pad ink, which is indelible and irritating to the tissues. It's useful for leaving an ineradicable mark for permanent identification.

ink under the skin as a form of tattooing. This isn't so much painful as disfiguring, and some people are vulnerable to this sort of threat. In some countries, the police tattoo their arrestees before release for ease of identification if ever they're arrested again. While an arrestee may have the mark removed by a plastic surgeon, this also leaves a scar, no matter how skilled the surgeon, and the police will be alert to a scar as evidence of previous contact, too. After WWII, for example, former members of the SS had their tattoos removed. These tattoos were always in the armpit, and Allied military police always examined the armpits for the tattoo or evidence of its removal.

Another category of irritants is the liniment family. Vicks, Ben-Gay, Infra-rub, and simple oil of wintergreen are extremely irritating when used on open wounds and mucus membranes. Applying a small amount to the nose, mouth, and genitals will cause a long-lasting irritation that takes hours to wear off. Applying it with a fingertip or cotton swab works as well as any other way. Only a small amount is necessary, because only the thin layer of the irritant next to the skin is effective.

Electricity

The use of electricity in torture is a Twentieth-Century innovation. This is quite different from the "electro-convulsive treatments" that were once used extensively to treat mental disorders. Some modern authorities confuse the two terms.[12] Psychiatric electro-shock is applying the electrodes to the temples and passing a current through the frontal lobes of the brain. This causes instant unconsciousness. Although electro-shock causes horrifying convulsions, unless these are suppressed by drugs that paralyze the muscles, the patient is unaware of it. This is why electro-shock has no value for interrogations.

Causing pain with electricity involves applying the current to other parts of the body. The reason that electricity's so effective is that many people have an extreme fear of it. Often, the mere threat of electricity will "crack" a subject. In other instances, pressing the stun gun's switch to make a spark crackle between the two test probes will immediately demoralize a subject.

There are many ways of using electricity. Direct current from a battery isn't as effective compared to alternating current, which causes far more pain. Alternating current also causes rapid and spasmodic muscular contractions.

The simplest way to apply electricity is to tape a common household electric cord to a wooden stick and bare the ends of the wire. When plugged in, the bare ends of the wire serve as electrodes to apply the current where the investigator wishes. Household 110-volt current can be dangerous, which makes it important to avoid the head, neck, chest, and spine.

In applying household current, pain can come from two causes. The current itself causes pain when passing through the tissues, often aggravated by involuntary and sharp muscular contractions. The current can also arc from imperfect contact, causing superficial burns on the skin. The burns cause far less pain than the flow of current. There are ways to lessen the risk of burns, as we'll see.

A cattle prod, or "hot shot," is another way. Cattle prods are available in hardware and feed stores for between fifteen and thirty dollars and run on dry cells. A transistorized circuit in the device boosts the voltage from the batteries and in doing so changes it to alternating current. Applying this to the skin can be very painful.

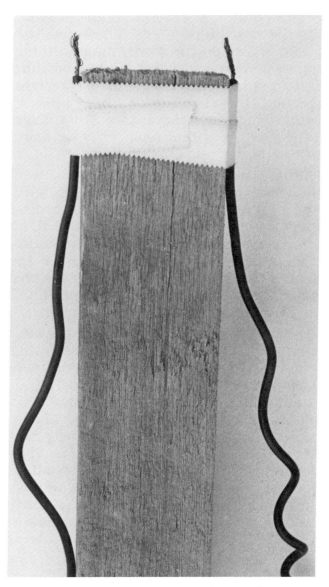

Common household electric cord taped to a wooden stick with the bare ends of the wire exposed.

The "stun gun," as used by both civilians and police, is the next highest level. These cost between twenty and eighty dollars, depending on the make. Some operate with a 9-volt carbon or alkaline cell. Manufacturers of the police model recommend rechargeable nickel-cadmium batteries, which deliver full voltage until they expire. Full voltage isn't important for the interrogator, who can use whatever battery he has on hand.

The stun gun delivers anywhere from twenty to fifty thousand volts at low amperage, which is supposedly fairly safe current to use. Regardless, it's important not to apply the electrodes to the head, spine, or chest near the heart. The stun gun electrodes can arc, leaving burns, and this is the sort of evidence that makes a charge of torture credible. The shape and spacing of the burns spell out "stun gun" to anyone who's familiar with them.

There are two techniques to avoid the characteristic burns. One is make sure that the electrodes are in good contact with the subject's skin. This can be difficult with a struggling subject. The other is to use conductive jelly, which is available in surgical supply houses and many pharmacies. Improvising conductive jelly requires emptying a tube of vegetable lubricant, such as K-Y, into a container, adding a tablespoon of salt. In use, it's important not to coat the subject's skin with it, but only the electrodes, as a layer of conductive jelly on the skin would cause the current to pass through it and short-circuit the subject. This would negate much of the effect.

There are also electrical muscle stimulators and other devices available only to people in the medical field. They cost much more than the simpler devices, but aren't a bit more effective for interrogation. A machine for applying psychiatric electro-shock, for

The "stun gun" is used by both civilians and police.

example, can cost thousands of dollars yet be no better than the seventy-dollar stun gun or twenty-dollar cattle prod.

The Subject Who Faints

Reviving an unconscious subject can be an ordeal, and the need is more common than many realize when the interrogation becomes intense. Some people faint easily, as a way of finding release from unbearable pressure. Others go into shock after severe pain. It's important for the interrogator to distinguish between simple fainting and physiological shock, because one's merely a nuisance, while the other's life-threatening.

Simple fainting occurs after a fright, and the subject loses consciousness. Reviving the subject usually requires only a douse of cold water or an ammonia inhalator.

Shock, on the other hand, happens after severe or prolonged pain, or serious physical injury, when the subject's resistance is overwhelmed. The skin is pale and sweaty, and breathing is shallow. Immediate attention requires keeping the subject prone but with the feet elevated. A blanket helps preserve body heat if there's danger of chilling. It may be necessary to use oxygen to ensure that the subject doesn't die or suffer brain damage from anoxia. Ammonia often helps, but in deep shock it may not work. It may be necessary to have the subject drink liquids once he regains consciousness. The investigating officer should not depend on his own skills to treat a subject in shock, unless he's had paramedic training.

TORTURE FOR THE EIGHTIES

Despite the advances made by humanitarians, the role of torture hasn't lessened by much. Torture continues to be a valuable tool where it's possible to use it. The important aspect for the investigating officer or police administrator is to ensure that torture remains only a tool, and doesn't become an end in itself for the gratification of a kinky personality.

Sources

1. *New York Times*, July 18, 1986.

2. *Physical Interrogation Techniques*, Richard W. Krousher, Port Townsend, WA, Loompanics Unlimited, 1985, p. 6.

3. *Secret Police*, Thomas Plate and Andrea Darvi, Garden City, New York, Doubleday & Company, 1981, p. 131.

4. *Ibid.*, p. 132.

5. *Ibid.*, p. 137.

6. *Ibid.*, p. 137.

7. *Physical Interrogation Techniques*, p. 23.

8. *Ibid.*, p. 17.

9. *Ibid.*, pp. 73-74.

10. *Secret Police*, p. 324.

11. *Ibid.*, p. 332.

12. *Ibid.*, p. 326. We find the term "electric shock treatment" used here, instead of "electric torture," which would be more appropriate.

THE GESTAPO
AND
OTHER SECRET POLICE

One of the most effective, and most misunderstood, security police organizations was the Gestapo. Let's examine it closely, because the Gestapo was a prototype secret police force, showing both the best and worst features of this sort of organization. This is why the Gestapo is worth studying, even though it's now history. We can learn a lot about interrogation and its place in investigation by studying how the Gestapo used and misused it.

The Gestapo was the victim of wartime propaganda which obscured its professionalism and terrifying effectiveness. The most widely-publicized branch of the Gestapo was "Office 4 B," in which Adolf Eichmann worked and which devoted itself to anti-Semitic persecutions. This is the least interesting branch of the Gestapo, because rounding up and deporting civilians is not a task that takes much skill.

The first point to examine is who made up the Gestapo. Contrary to some of the wartime propaganda accounts, Gestapo agents were not recruited from the violent wards of mental hospitals, nor were they released criminals. They were all professional police officers. Mueller, their chief, had been an inspector with the Karlsruhe police. The

Gestapo typically recruited its officers from the ranks of experienced criminal investigators.

A counter-espionage investigation is very much like a criminal investigation, and many of the methods are exactly the same. An experienced criminal investigator can easily break in and work counter-espionage.

In both fields, physical evidence plays a part, but interrogation of suspects and developing informers is even more important. Working "undercover" agents against a criminal enterprise or a spy ring entails the same set of skills

Fundamentally, the Gestapo was a counter-espionage and counter-subversive police, very much like that of most other countries in the world. The Gestapo was originally the Prussian State Police, until the Nazis were voted into power in 1933. The character of the organization then changed somewhat, and one of the little-known facts about the Gestapo is that Hermann Goering was its head for a short time at the outset of the Nazi era.

The role of the Gestapo was confusing to outsiders, partly because of the peculiarities of the Nazi regime. The National Socialist Party duplicated many arms of the German government. The "Waffen-SS" was the party's army, for example. The well-known "Sicherheitsdeinst" (translation: Security Service; pronunciation: seeker-hites-deenst) was the party's secret police. During the Nazi regime, the two organizations grew closer, partly because of avid empire-building by Heinrich Himmler, head of the SS. In 1943, the marriage was complete, and the Gestapo and the Sicherheitsdienst were one and the same, merged into the "Reichssicherheitshauptamt," one of those awful compound nouns ("Government Security Head Office") which are characteristic of the German language. In 1944, the SD absorbed the Abwehr (military intelligence), its last rival, and was finally the undisputed master of both the intelligence and counter-espionage efforts.

The Gestapo dealt with anything which might be a threat to the security of the state. This covered resistance and underground movements, sedition, dissidence, and foreign-induced espionage. The history of the Nazi regime reveals that there were factions within the armed forces and the civil government opposed to Adolf Hitler. There were several attempts to assassinate him, the last of which almost succeeded. The most tangible and violent result of this attempt was that many of the participants and their sympathizers were rounded up and executed. Some were the victims of summary courts-martial, and others went to formal trials and were sentenced to death, as was Admiral Canaris, head of the Abwehr.

There have been many accounts of underground movements and other efforts against the Nazi occupation during World War II. Some of these were purely indigenous in origin, and only later derived help from foreign powers. The British set up a special organization, the "Special Operations Executive," to plan and carry out sabotage against the German occupation forces.₁ In many ways this organization performed the same tasks as the present-day CIA and KGB in their covert support of insurrectionists in various countries. The S.O.E. was not alone, as other Allied countries had their own sabotage organizations which worked with and supported underground movements throughout Europe.

The Gestapo was essentially a defensive force, but Gestapo contingents followed the conquering armies to help consolidate the annexed territories. Each occupied country had its Gestapo office. There also were other arms of German Intelligence and counter-espionage operating. One of the curses of Twentieth-Century governments is the extraordinarily wasteful duplication and overlapping of similar organizations. We see a lot of that in the United States, but even the supposedly "efficient" Germans were far from immune to this.

One of the most prominent counter-espionage organizations was a branch of the "Abwehr." This service, under Admiral Wilhelm Canaris, had its aces and superstars, just as did the Gestapo, and we can only speculate how much efficiency was lost because they did not work on the same team. For our discussion, let's consider them as the same team, because they had the same purpose: safeguarding the Nazi regime.

The popular image of the Gestapo agent comes to us from wartime propaganda. The snarling and jack-booted Gestapo officer who threatens his captive as a preliminary to brutal torture is the stereotype, with few real-life counterparts. More typical of the approach to a captive is this account by a member of the Czech Resistance who described his arrest by the Gestapo. [2]

"One day, while I was at home, the bell rang, and this well-dressed man told me that he was from the Gestapo and asked me to accompany him to his office to straighten out a minor problem. In the car, he told me that his investigation into the resistance had turned up my name, and that he'd appreciate it if I would tell him what I knew of it. He said that he was trying to help me get out of an embarrassing situation, especially as my family was one of the most prominent in Prague and he did not want to tarnish the family name. At his office, he continued to be polite, offering me cigarettes and tea, but I told him that I knew nothing about the resistance. He did not get angry, or threaten me with torture. He repeated his concern about helping me, and told me that if I was cooperative, he could do a lot to see that the charges against me would be minimal ones. I continued to refuse him and wound up in Thereseinstadt."

From this account, we can infer a lot. First, the main effort of the Gestapo was to obtain willing cooperation, not inflict sadistic tortures. All over the world, honey catches more flies than vinegar, and if the soft approach would work, it was the best method.

Another point is that this resistance worker was from a prominent Czech family, and even under the German occupation, this meant status. If he'd been a Jew, or a foreigner, his treatment might have been much harsher, especially after he refused to cooperate.

Finally, the "nice guy" treatment was productive often enough for the Gestapo to use it as the method of choice. An agent in danger of being executed knows that he can strike a "deal" with his captors, and it's often a great temptation to trade the lives of fellow agents for one's own. The Gestapo exploited this obvious fact diligently.

The "nice guy" treatment didn't always work. A lot depended on the captive, and the personality and style of the interrogator. Some Gestapo interrogators didn't have the patience for subtleties, and placed their faith in coercive measures. A spy or subversive in their hands could expect severities.

The Gestapo, well-organized as it was, had procedures laid out for what was known as "rigorous interrogation" and "especially rigorous interrogation." These involved carefully counted lashes, and required the presence of a doctor to see that the subject's health wasn't endangered. The policies laid out in the manual weren't always strictly followed.

Some of the wartime propaganda was based on fact. In some instances, Gestapo agents employed physical torture to extract information. This wasn't to obtain confessions, as under even German law extorted confessions were inadmissible, but to extract information that the suspect would otherwise not divulge, such as names of confederates. The methods used were extreme, and some of the Gestapo's suspects died in the process.[3]

In these extreme instances, a lot depended on the intiative of the interrogator. Some used kicks and punches to persuade the suspect to talk. Others, more technically inclined, would use mechanical or electrical means of inflicting pain. One method was to immerse the captive in a bath-tub of ice water. Another was to squeeze the testicles with a clamp. Yet another was an expedient known as the "telephone." This made use of an army field telephone with a hand-cranked magneto providing the ringing current. Attaching the wires to sensitive areas of the body produced severe pain when the interrogator spun the crank. The usual practice was to attach the leads to the genitals.

This method was so spectacularly successful that others copied it after the war. The French used electricity for interrogations during the Algerian War. The CIA provided portable electrical interrogation sets for use by the political police of client states.

Disposing of the plethora of captured spies was not much of a problem. The standard method was to exploit a spy for as long as possible. If the suspect continued to cooperate, revealing his associates and procedures, he had a lease on life. Sometimes, this affair could become quite involved. The suspect would be "played back" to his home office under Gestapo control. He would continue to keep in contact with the spymasters in London, sending his messages under Gestapo supervision, and asking for parachute drops of other agents and replenishment of supplies. The well-known "Operation North Pole" was a superb example of playing back captured agents. This was mainly an Abwehr operation, although there was some cooperation from the Gestapo.

"Playing back" required active cooperation from the subjects. Typically, agents were given "security checks," code words to be inserted into messages as signals that they were not operating under duress. Omitting the security check signalled that the agent had been caught and was being played back. The Gestapo was able to get willing cooperation from agents who told all, including revealing the security check. A typical Gestapo operation rounded up agents, parachuted supplies, and entire networks of spies.4

The fate of captured agents varied. Some survived the war. There were, however, too many for the Gestapo to house. Conviction by court-martial was not hard to obtain. Physical evidence alone was usually enough. Anyone caught with a code-pad, short-wave radio, or a weapon would be hard put to explain these away to the satisfaction of the court. Some agents were informally killed, "shot while trying to escape." Others went before firing squads. Yet others received the treatment handed out to "subhumans," lethal injections and immediate cremation.5 Yet others were hanged on hooks, dying by strangulation.6

The uncomfortable fact is that the secret police of the "totalitarian" and the "democratic" countries work in similar ways. The treatment they get in the media depends entirely upon who wins the war. The loser has all of his activities examined and laid out in the least flattering manner. The winner wraps his activities in a veil of secrecy. Typically, secret service records are kept classified for many years, and sometimes permanently. Occasionally, carefully "sanitized" versions are released to friendly historians. The secret interrogations and secret executions usually remain forever secret.

In rare instances in the Western countries, a former agent will "tell all" in a book published as fiction. One such is a little-known, but excellent book, *The Officer From Special Branch,* by Tom Lilley. This book deals with the British response to the Malayan disturbances, and was published in the United States, not Britain. This is significant, because in Britain, the "Official Secrets Act" allows the government to suppress books and articles that touch upon "classified" matters or other material that the government doesn't want revealed. Publication outside the country is the only way to put out such a book, and the fact that this was done lends credence to the book's authenticity. "Tom Lilley" is probably a pen-name, and judging from the book, he seems to have been a police officer or army counter-terrorist specialist during the period. The writing style is utilitarian, descriptive, but not great literature. It's a rational and coherent account of the ruthless methods the British occupation forces used against the insurgents in Malaya.

The code of morality laid out in the book is one of pure expediency. Success is the only criterion, and complaints about the immorality of treachery and entrapment are merely tiresome babblings of the naive and uninformed. The episodes described in the book reveal techniques of double-cross that are used against insurgent movements everywhere. Indeed, reading this book places the current Northern Ireland War into proper perspective.7

Secret police everywhere tend to share the same methods. At this point, it will be useful to lay out what, exactly, makes a "secret police" or "security police" and how it's different from the regular police. First, it's obvious that the "secret" police is usually not secret at all. Everyone knows it exists, as the names such as Gestapo, KGB, SAVAK, and DINA are almost household words in their respective countries.

One distinction between the secret police and the regular police is that the secret police tends to operate without what most of us would consider "due process." There are warrantless searches and arrests, wiretapping and other surveillance, detention without trial, and "administrative" dispositions to cases.8 A network of undercover agents and informers blankets the country, and there's an air of having to watch what you say.

This leads us to the next commonly-accepted distinction. Secret police officers tend to have jurisdiction over acts that would not be considered illegal elsewhere. In most of the Western countries, membership in an opposition party is legal, and even part of the "system." Publishing news and views contrary to government policy is also protected under a constitution or legal tradition. Holding meetings is also a protected activity. Not so in the world of the secret police. While we have ample evidence of secret police surveillance of opposition political parties in the Western countries, the secret police have to be discreet, and usually serve only as an intelligence-gathering arm of the government rather than as a weapon of counter-attack against the opposition.

Secret police focus on espionage and on political crimes, "crimes against the state," rather than on street crimes, those defined in the penal code. However, what constitutes a "crime against the state" and therefore the concern of the secret police depends on the country. Much white-collar crime, for example, isn't even covered by the penal code in the United States. In Soviet Russia, most white-collar crimes are serious offenses, and under the jurisdiction of the KGB. Some carry the death penalty.

Another feature of secret police is that it often is not just the defender of the state, but of the person who is the head of state. The secret police becomes that individual's personal police force. This is characteristic of autocratic regimes, where the dictator may even feel, as Louis XIV did, that *"L'etat, c'est moi"* (The state is me). In a dictatorship, they often are one and the same, and the state does not survive the death of the dictator in the same form. A good example is Franco's Spain, which changed much after the Caudillo's demise.

Yet another feature to distinguish the secret police is that it operates without statutory authority.[9] This is especially true of the political and security police organizations of the British Commonwealth countries. The British Security Service, DI-5, for example, is not authorized by any formal law, and its funds are part of the "secret vote."[10] This isn't too surprising, because one of its functions is to monitor certain political parties considered threats to the security of the state.[11] The differences between DI-5 and its counterparts in the more repressive countries is what it does with the information. In

Britain, it isn't a crime to belong to an opposition or fringe political party. This is why DI-5 keeps a low profile, and operates with great discretion.

A very important practical distinction for the people working in a secret police organization is that the pay and/or benefits are greater than those of the regular police. Salary is usually higher, as a start. Fringe benefits usually accompany the higher salaries. They may include a "company car," privileged housing, access to special shops, unrestricted travel, and other miscellaneous benefits that come from being part of an undeniably elite organization. In some instances the salary is partly or completely exempt from taxation. With hidden funds, the secret police can do a lot to raise the living standards of its loyal members.

There's also the ugly prospect of corruption. In certain countries, membership in the secret police is not only a license to kill, but a license to loot.12 This is one of the fringe benefits. Agents may expropriate the property of their arrestees. Typically, this is characteristic of the third-world secret policeman, and not allowed in the ranks of well-trained and tightly-disciplined organizations such as the Gestapo, FBI, and KGB. A rule of thumb is that in countries where the regular police practice institutionalized corruption, the secret police follow suit.

The fundamental fact seems to be that secret police organizations vary in quality, as well as in orientation. Some of the worst, such as the Chilean "DINA," are positively sleazy in both personnel and methods of operation.13 The most notorious seem to be merely personal goon squads for the person in power, rather than a force defending the state. Whatever the purpose, many of the methods are surprisingly similar.

Sources

1. *Set Europe Ablaze,* E.H. Cookridge, New York, T.Y. Crowell, Inc., 1966.

2. Related to the author by the person involved, who later fled the Communist regime in Czechoslovakia and came to the United States.

3. *Set Europe Ablaze,* p. 16.

4. *Ibid.,* p. 183.

5. *Ibid.,* p. 185.

6. *Ibid.,* p. 244.

7. *The Officer From Special Branch,* Tom Lilley, New York, Doubleday and Company, 1971.

8. *Secret Police,* Thomas Plate and Andrea Darvi, Garden City, New York, Doubleday & Company, 1981, pp. 9-10.

9. *Ibid.,* p. 34.

10. *The Circus,* Nigel West, New York, Stein and Day, 1983, p. 19.

11. *Ibid.,* pp. 16, 17, 18, and 22.

12. *Secret Police,* p. 40.

13. *Ibid.,* starting with page 1. Much of this book uses examples from the history of DINA to illustrate the points regarding unsavory security police organizations. The Pinochet regime in Chile seems to have furnished a lot of material in just a few years for organizations such as Amnesty International.

SOVIET INTERROGATION AND "BRAINWASHING"

There's probably more myth and mis-information about this subject than there is legitimate and verifiable information. The alleged ability of Communist interrogators to bend anyone to their will implies that resistance is useless, and that the strongest person can withstand the pressure for a limited time. This is the legend, and almost certainly untrue.

Let's make a start at untangling fact from fiction. How do we get our information about the more unsavory aspects of the Soviet Union, and how reliable is it?

There's a segment of opinion in this country that's willing to believe anything negative about the Soviet Union, to accept it at face value. At the same time, these people dismiss anything positive as "propaganda" or "disinformation."

One reason that "brainwashing" has become such a controversial and fascinating subject is that it meets several definite and deep needs. An American military man who does something dishonorable while captured by the other side may face a court-martial if he returns to the United States. Claiming that he was brainwashed is a useful cop-out. It allows him to repudiate a confession he signed to obtain better rations, or excuses his betrayal of other servicemen and fellow-prisoners.

On a higher level, the concept of brainwashing serves a national purpose, too. It undermines the credibility of any confession by American servicemen captured by the other side. An American officer captured by the Communists during the Korean war, Colonel Frank H. Schwable, confessed to having taken part in a "germ warfare" program. Upon his release, he repudiated his confession.1

An important point to understand is that a military man asked to "confess" to certain acts faces the same situation regardless of the truth of his "confession."

(1) He's under pressure to confess. This pressure may be in the form of the carrot or the stick, or both. Cooperating with his captors can gain him certain benefits, such as extra food, permission to write letters home and to receive mail from his family, better living quarters, early release, etc. There can also be outright coercion, such as confinement in a cramped, dark, and uncomfortable cell as punishment for non-cooperation. Other measures include being forced to stand at attention for many hours, forced marches in freezing cold weather, and not being allowed to sleep. Sometimes, physical violence is part of the coercion.2

(2) The "confession" will harm his country, regardless of whether it's true or false. If it's false, the captive's instrumental in preparing an accusation against his country, one that will be useful in Communist propaganda. If it's true, he'll be revealing classified information to the enemy.

(3) The final problem comes if and when the captive returns home. It can be awkward to admit that he confessed for a couple of packs of cigarettes

or bowls of rice. It's convenient to claim that he caved
in after extraordinary pressure, treatment that
robbed him of his will to resist and part of his
personality.

THE GROWTH OF A MYTH

The spectacular "Moscow Trials" of the late 1930s
provided a definite turning-point in our perception
of the Soviet ability to extract confessions. The
problem is aggravated by the fact that, even today, we
don't know the full story of these trials. The official
Soviet line was that certain high-level Soviet officials
had plotted a coup d'etat against the regime, had
been found out, and put on trial for treason. The
amazing spectacle of a parade of renowned high
Soviet officials testifying against themselves in these
trials gave rise to the idea that they'd been forced to
confess, although the means were not clear at the
time.

Confusing the issue was the allegation that came
out after WWII that Heydrich, the Nazi
Sicherheitsdienst leader, had instigated a plot to
frame these Soviet officials. This version of the
events was that Heydrich wanted to eviscerate the
Soviet leadership, especially that of the armed forces,
by taking advantage of Stalin's alleged paranoia.
Heydrich allegedly leaked information about
collusion between the Soviet General Staff and the
Nazi High Command to a source that would get the
information back to Stalin. If this version is true, it
was spectacularly successful. The leadership of the
Soviet military, including the well-known and
capable Marshal Mikhail Tukhachevsky, were
interrogated, tried, convicted, and executed, along
with so many co-conspirators that about two-thirds

178

of the senior officers were executed or imprisoned. This supposedly accounted for the gap in leadership that led to the Soviets' poor performance in the war against Finland in 1939-1940.

We find a contrary view in former American Ambassador Joseph Davies' book, *Mission to Moscow*. Davies, an American conservative, described the events of the Moscow Trials in a way that left little doubt about the defendants' guilt. Although it wasn't possible to attack Davies on his ideology, as he was a staunch conservative, some Americans, after the start of the cold war, claimed that Davies had been duped by Stalin.

In 1940, the ex-communist author, Arthur Koestler, wrote a novel, *Darkness at Noon*, based on his perception of the Moscow Trails. Understandably, because Koestler was anti-communist at the time, this novel presented the view that the main character was utterly innocent and the victim of ruthless manipulation by the totalitarian state. This was fiction, but it had as much impact on our views as did factual reports.

After WWII, several events enlarged our view of Soviet methods of obtaining confessions. The 1949 trial of Cardinal Mindszenty, in Hungary, showed a high official of the Catholic Church confessing to espionage. An American, Robert Vogeler, was arrested by the Communists and put on trial for espionage. At the time, well before the U-2 incident, most Americans believed that espionage was a dirty trick undertaken only by the disreputable regimes such as the Nazis and Communists. Clean-cut Americans would never stoop so low as to spy on other nations, especially those with whom we were not at war. By this reasoning, it was obvious that something had been done to Mr. Vogeler's mind to make him confess falsely.

The novel, *Darkness at Noon*, enjoyed a rebirth and its greatest period of success. It became an American television play, and a paperback book. In 1949, George Orwell's novel *1984*, came out. Orwell wrote about a futuristic totalitarian secret police that crushed everyone under its heel. The main character, Winston Smith, found himself arrested on a variety of charges, among which was prohibited fornication with a woman. Illicit sex was not allowed under the rules of this regime. The interrogation involved physical and mental rigors, including the full range of psychiatric treatment known at the time. Winston Smith received electro-shock treatments. He and his girl friend were both slated for execution at a later date, to suit the convenience of the secret police.

The Korean War which immediately followed this brought the image of brainwashing into the headlines. "Brainwashing" is a term that originated with the Chinese Communists, as a synonym for "thought reform," a way of ideological conversion. As part of the consolidation of the revolution, the Chinese Communists faced the problem of converting masses of people to their way of thinking.

This was a fairly straightforward matter. The regime set up discussion groups that placed a premium on "self-criticism," using peer pressure to persuade individuals to toe the party line. Backing up the effort of voluntary mind reform is the power of the state, with a firing squad reserved for anyone deemed "counter-revolutionary." There's nothing dark or mysterious about this. It works, and works well. The acceptance of compulsory birth control and abortion by the Chinese is evidence of the method's effectiveness in promoting profound social reforms.

American intelligence specialists, however, speculated on the possibility that the Soviets had developed drugs that would render a person subservient to an interrogator's will. During WWII, the OSS had issued pills containing the active ingredient of marijuana as an aid to interrogation. This had many shortcomings, the main one being that it didn't work, but there was always the prospect that someone else had been successful. The whole project eventually turned out to be a false lead.3

Fiction, however, seemed to be always ahead of fact. The appearance of Richard Condon's novel, *The Manchurian Candidate*, gave us a picture of terrifyingly efficient Communist mind-manipulators. The plot was that Stalin devised a plan, back in 1936, to brainwash Americans and use them to return to their country to be unwitting Soviet agents. To this end, a team of Chinese and Soviet Russian psychologists worked over a captured American patrol during the Korean War, using drugs and hypnosis to change their personalities during a two-day period of captivity. They were then returned to no-man's-land and released to make their way back to American lines with no recollection of what had been done to them. Years later, the stepfather of one of the returned soldiers makes a try at the U.S. Presidency, and the brainwashed soldier aids in the effort by committing murders at the orders of the Soviet spy network.

Although this was pure science fiction, the *Manchurian Candidate* caught on and became a best-seller and a motion picture, starring Frank Sinatra and Lawrence Harvey. The theme became so popular that "Manchurian Candidate" became a generic term for an espionage or sabotage agent under absolute control, even though there hasn't been a real-life counterpart.

The downing of the U-2 aerial reconnaissance aircraft in May, 1960, was a watershed event in several different areas, and profoundly affected our history. First, it showed that the U.S. government used methods that it condemned in others. Secondly, the events showed the spectacular failure of a cover story used to explain the downing of the aircraft. The Soviet government withheld the news of the capture of Powers, the pilot, to allow the American government time to bring forth what turned out to be an obvious lie. The U-2 was recovered intact enough to allow the Soviets to put the components on exhibit for the press, its own people, and as evidence in the trial of the pilot.

Francis Gary Powers, the pilot, was put on trial for espionage, and the trial was covered by the Western media. There could be no claim that the Soviets had manipulated Powers' mind, because the physical evidence made it unnecessary. The captured cameras, silenced pistol, poisoned needle, and other apparatus of the spy trade were convincing, even to Americans who saw it only through the eyes of the media. Powers' conviction was a foregone conclusion because it was what is called in this country an "open-and-shut case."

Powers' own account, after his release, was simply that the Soviets offered him a deal. They had the evidence to convict him, and the sentence he'd receive depended mostly on the attitude he displayed before the court. If he appeared unrepentant and defiant, they'd throw the book at him. If he showed remorse, he'd get leniency. This was an offer he couldn't refuse, and he confessed.

A possibly deciding factor in his decision might have been viewing the wreckage of his aircraft. At the time, there was an unsubstantiated rumor that the CIA considered the pilot's death preferable to capture and interrogation, which is why he was issued a poison needle. Another part to this rumor

182

was that the self-destruct device fitted to the plane had an instantaneous fuse instead of a delayed timer, as the pilots had been told. Apparently, Powers had had some dark suspicions about this, because he did not activate the self-destruction device when he bailed out. If in fact the device was set to go off instantly, to destroy the pilot as well as the aircraft, it would have been a very persuasive means for the Soviets to use to convince the pilot that his employers had planned to forsake him all along. Such physical evidence would be far more effective than any mind-manipulation technique.

A few years later, Greville Wynne, a British spy, was arrested by the Soviets. He too stood trial in Moscow, and had been caught in circumstances so compromising that his government could not claim that he'd been framed. As with Powers, Wynne showed no evidence of having been mentally raped by sinister secret policemen, and his conviction was not surprising. Both Powers and Wynne didn't serve out their sentences, because they were exchanged for Soviet spies held in Western prisons.

With all that, there is such a thing as forced confession Soviet-style, although this may be a misnomer because similar methods work equally well in the West. We'll trace the development of "brainwashing" and its modern-day implementation in the next chapter.

Sources

1. *Brainwashing*, Edward Hunter, New York, Pyramid Books, 1958, p. 8. However, see pp. 178-179 in the book, *A Higher Form of Killing*, Robert Harris and Jeremy Paxman, New York, Hill and Wang, 1982. An independent report claimed that the United

States did use germ warfare in Korea. Even today, it's not possible to state categorically what the facts really were. As the discussion shows, however, the facts are not very relevant to the captive under pressure to confess.

2. *Ibid.*, pp. 201-205.

3. *A Higher Form of Killing*, p. 226.

SOVIET INTERROGATION AND "BRAINWASHING" PART II

The Soviets and their allies in the Eastern Bloc Countries have developed a systematic way of extracting confessions, and even forcing a change in the personality, by a process often known as "brainwashing." This is the allegation of Edward Hunter, a former CIA agent who wrote the book by that name.[1]

This is vaguely comparable to what we call "behavioral modification" in this country. It depends on semi-starvation, isolation, drugs, and long sessions with an interrogator and sometimes a peer group to effect the change, which may be temporary or permanent. Its permanence depends on how well and how frequently the behavior change is reinforced once established. Experience with released victims of "brainwashing" shows that once they're away from the people and conditions that caused the change, they usually shake off the behavior pattern within weeks or months. The after-effects may persist for much longer.[2]

Those who remain within the closed society are much more likely to retain the lessons taught. This is because of continual reinforcement and possibly fear of the consequences of backsliding.

"Brainwashing" is really a learning experience. The subject learns what his interrogator wants, and learns that providing it is less painful and more rewarding than not cooperating.

The critical question is whether brainwashing is a truly irresistable method or not. If it is, was it applied to Allied prisoners of war in Korea? There's been a lot of rhetoric about this, and sorting the facts from the fiction is a worthwhile task.

Let's start with some statistics, to sketch the outline of the events. Of 7,190 American prisoners, 2,730 died while captive. Of the others, about 13% were strong collaborators, some caving in after only a few minutes of questioning. About the same proportion were hard-line resisters. The rest were not as spectacularly committed, and their behavior varied from moderate collaboration to moderate resistance. Twenty-one Americans refused repatriation at the end of hostilities. Some of the collaborators had brutalized their fellow-captives on behalf of their captors, and about 75 had apparently accepted instructions to return to the United States to spy for the Communists. They were equipped with codes and instructions to lay low for a period before activation.[3]

British soldiers were also subjected to indoctrination, having sent the Gloucester Regiment to fight in Korea. There were 980 soldiers captured. One decided to refuse repatriation at the end of the war. About two-thirds were totally innocent of any sort of collaboration. The 4% who came back stating that they were Communists were significant in that most of them had been Communists before they were captured.[4]

In the Korean War, there were also 229 members of the Turkish Battalion captured and held by the Communists. None died in captivity, although almost half were wounded when taken, and none committed even the slightest act of collaboration.[5]

The evidence shows that Allied troops captured in Korea were not "brainwashed."6 The treatment they received was more in the nature of indoctrination and trying to play some prisoners off against each other, than systematic personality alteration. During the heat of the war, and immediately after, it was convenient to claim that Americans who espoused the "Communist Line" had had their personalities altered. This was convenient for the government in explaining away confessions of germ warfare and other atrocities. It was convenient for any confessors who returned to the United States: "The devil made me do it."

The contrast between the behaviors of American prisoners and Turkish ones is startling. It would be convenient and reassuring to conclude that the Turks fared better because the Communist captors reserved their main efforts for their American captives. Unfortunately, there's no evidence to support this conclusion. All were in the same harsh environment.

This implies some uncomfortable conclusions about ourselves and our morale. Americans simply were not up to it, and easily played off by Communist guards. The captors found that an appeal to Americans' desires for creature comforts and special privilege would bring about a certain number of "converts." Promising better food and warmer clothing gained results. Some prisoners betrayed their country for a few material advantages. Others betrayed their buddies, becoming informers for the Communists.

The experience of American POWs in Korea brought about a significant change in the attitude of the American government. Eisenhower was President at the end of the Korean War, and as a former military man he was very concerned over the behavior of American soldiers while in captivity. A military board, after studying the problem, devised a "code of conduct" to guide American servicemen in case of capture. [7]

Basically, the code forbids surrender while the individual or unit still has the means to fight, and encourages resistance and escape. Servicemen are also forbidden to give "parole" that they will not attempt to escape in return for special privileges. They're obligated to avoid giving the enemy information beyond their names, ranks, and serial numbers, and also enjoined not to inform on their fellow captives. Above all, they're forbidden to provide the enemy with "confessions." They're also obligated to maintain a chain of command and obey lawful orders.

In practice, this is workable, but has its limits. First, it's not proof against torture, and prisoners may be compelled to cooperate with their captors by means of physical torture.[8] Prolonged incarceration can impair health, weakening the prisoner's power to resist.

For fairly short-term captivity, the code of conduct can help see the captives through. Unfortunately it's no better than those who use it, and the stress of captivity as the days go on without release can challenge the resolve of many. The captors can tell the prisoners that they've been abandoned by their country, and inevitably some will believe this version.

Resistance is also difficult in marginal situations. An injured prisoner may find that medical attention is linked to his "cooperating" with his captors. One American Corporal sustained frostbite in his left hand and right foot. This developed into gangrene, and the reaction of his captors was that injured Koreans had to have priority in the scarce medical facilities. The interrogator made it clear to him that he would have to qualify for medical care by "proving" himself. This meant confessing and informing on his fellow prisoners.9

The belief that Communists possessed arcane power to mold minds beyond anything known in the Western world persisted. When the Soviets captured a U-2 aircraft in 1960, they also captured the pilot alive. Francis Gary Powers, pilot of the doomed plane, survived unharmed, and was to stand trial in Moscow. Allen Dulles, then head of the Central Intelligence Agency, felt that Powers had been brainwashed before the trial.10

The picture was not as dramatic as that, as we saw in the last chapter. Powers underwent sixty-one days of more-or-less conventional police-style interrogation by Soviet authorities. It was clear from the start that he'd been caught red-handed and that the Russians were angry over the flight and displeased with him. The Soviets needed no confession to convict him. As an adult and former military man, he was aware that the possible penalty for espionage was death by firing squad. The court-appointed defense attorney made it clear to Powers that his sentence would depend very heavily on the attitude he displayed to the court. If he showed repentance, the judges would be more inclined to impose a lighter sentence.11

The Powers case was not typical either of the treatment handed out to Korean war prisoners or to the defendants in the Moscow trials of the late 1930s. Powers was not given the mass-production treatment, nor did he experience the severities meted out to the political prisoners by Stalin's OGPU. Let's examine exactly what comprised the much-feared methods of the Soviet Secret Police.

Basically, these were standard police methods, known before the Soviet government took over

Russia, and also practiced by police worldwide.[12] There were several techniques, usually used together, to harass a suspect into confessing.

One was imposition of physical discomfort. Keeping a subject handcuffed, or tied in an uncomfortable position for hours or even days, was common. Added to this would be refusal of permission to use the toilet, refusal of food and water, and sometimes extremes of temperature.

Another technique was not letting the prisoner rest. Keeping him awake answering questions posed by relays of interrogators soon confused a subject deprived of sleep.

Endless interrogation to produce confusion was another tactic, which fit in well with sleep deprivation. Asking the same set of questions repeatedly will eventually produce some contradictions, which the interrogator can bring up to the subject, suggesting deception. Once he makes the initial breakthrough, the interrogator can continue claiming that the subject is lying, even if he has to fabricate contradictions.

Captivity and close interrogation of this sort soon demonstrate to the subject that his interrogator can control whether he's comfortable or uncomfortable. His interrogator can decree when he's fed and given drink. He can withhold cigarettes, food, clothing, and other comforts and necessities. This soon gives the interrogator the aura of omnipotence because the subject is himself so helpless. It's therefore not surprising that the subject soon realizes the need to please the interrogator.

Isolated from his family and friends, and anyone else who may help him, the prisoner is utterly dependent on the captor's good will. After a period of harsh measures, he's vulnerable to the delusion that the interrogator's concerned for his welfare and wants only to help him. The police officer plays an emotional game with the prisoner, trading on the subject's will for survival, and convinces the subject that it's in his best interest to cooperate. At this point, emotionally exhausted, the subject actively attempts to give the interrogator what he wants. He'll confess willingly in an effort to please his captor. He'll accuse himself, seeking approval.

BRAINWASHING, FACT AND FICTION

We can see from all this that "brainwashing" exists, but has been exaggerated beyond all reason. In reality, very few people have been through a severe regime of brainwashing. The reason is purely practical. It's too expensive and time-consuming. Assigning a team of interrogators to only one subject ties up a number of experienced police officers who might be better employed on other duties. Interrogating a subject in this intensive manner for many weeks takes a lot of manpower.

Korean POWs were not brainwashed. Those who collaborated with the enemy did so out of selfishness and weakness of character. The few Communist political captives who did undergo "brainwashing" actually received a treatment very similar to the forced interrogations imposed by other police forces on our unhappy planet.

This is both good news and bad news. Good because there's nothing mysterious or incomprehensible about brainwashing. Bad because it's so common. Bad because almost anyone can break down and confess under this prolonged treatment. Human beings are sometimes startlingly weak. It takes very little to force a confession.

191

Sources

1. *Brainwashing*, Edward Hunter, New York, Pyramid Books, 1958.

2. *Techniques of Persuasion*, J.A.C. Brown, Baltimore, Maryland, Penguin Books, 1963, pp. 283-284.

3. *Ibid.*, pp. 255-263.

4. *Ibid.*, pp. 263-264.

5. *Ibid.*, p. 264.

6. *Ibid.*, p. 265.

7. *Prisoner of War Resistance*, FM 21-78, Department of the Army Manual. Commercially reprinted by Paladin Press.

8. *Ibid.*, p. 20.

9. *Behavior Modification*, Richard Camellion, Boulder, Colorado, Paladin Press, 1978, pp. 46-50.

10. *Mayday*, Michael R. Beschloss, New York, Harper & Row, Publishers, 1986, p. 335.

11. *Ibid.*, p. 328.

12. *Techniques of Persuasion*, p. 268.

INTERROGATION FAILURES

Interrogators don't always get their way. Despite claims or implications of perfection, some subjects are too resistant for their interrogators. The methods themselves are imperfect. The interrogators, despite their superior knowledge, are only human. It's hard to find a frank admission of this in the books devoted to interrogation and allied subjects. The authors describe the techniques as if they work all the time. They also describe their many successes. Rarely do they describe their failures.

There are basically two types of failures. One is the failure to obtain a confession or meaningful information. This is usually the result of inept interrogation, but the Miranda Decision has provided a common excuse.

The second serious problem with any interrogation technique is the prospect of extracting a confession from an innocent person. There's no documentation as to how often this happens, but there have been some notable instances. Opinion is divided on this point, and the political orientation of the person doing the evaluation plays a major role in some instances. For example, an American describing the brainwashing that took place with POWs captured by the Communists in Korea will most likely maintain that the prisoners were innocent, and forced to confess to fabricated charges such as using germ warfare.

Similarly, it's a foregone conclusion, when an American is arrested in the Soviet Union, that the United States Government will maintain that he's innocent and the charges are trumped up. The treatment he gets from the KGB will get close scrutiny. We can only imagine what the Soviets say when one of their agents is arrested by the FBI here.

We do have some well-documented criminal cases, which offer us good opportunities to examine why and when interrogations go wrong, and how these failures affect the rest of the criminal justice system.

THE WYLIE-HOFFERT MURDER CASE

In August, 1963, a sensational and brutal crime took place in New York City. In April of the following year, the wrong man was arrested for it, and he confessed his guilt to the police. A close look at this case will give an indication of the problems with police interrogation, even in as open a society as the United States and with one of the most professional police agencies in the world.

Two young career girls, Janice Wylie, (niece of author Phillip Wylie), and Emily Hoffert, shared an apartment on the East Side of Manhattan. The killer attacked Janice Wylie as she came out of the shower, after surreptitiously entering the apartment. He knocked her unconscious, tied her up and raped her, then killed her with a knife taken from the kitchen. When Emily Hoffert arrived home, he repeated the process with her.1 Many months passed without an arrest for these murders, and the pressure on the police to make progress was intense. The two girls were white and one, Janice Wylie, had articulate relatives with powerful friends. If they had been black and poor, and lived in the ghetto, the case would not have attracted such long-lasting attention.

A suspect, George Whitmore, was arrested on another matter. During his interrogation, the detectives somehow got the idea that he might be connected with the Wylie-Hoffert murders. The interrogation lasted for twenty hours, and in the end the suspect confessed. The confession, with 61 typewritten pages of details, told explicitly how he committed the murders. The account gave a step-by-step, blow-by-blow narrative which was convincing to the police, the District Attorney, and eventually to a judge and jury.

There was one fatal flaw in the case: Whitmore was totally innocent of that crime. Although he had a record, and in fact was eventually to be convicted of other crimes he committed around that time, he had not committed the Wylie-Hoffert murders. An investigation disclosed that Whitmore was in Wildwood, New Jersey, on the day that those two murders were committed. Thus it was eventually established beyond doubt that he could not have done them.

Another man, Richard Robles, was "turned over" by a friend who was informing for the police. The evidence against him was solid, and he, too, was convicted.

The problem was that the Whitmore investigation could have, after so much careful work and diligent interrogation, produced a totally false confession. Even the investigative keys, the closely-held details of the crimes, were correct in the confession.

No documentation exists of what really went on in the interrogation room. The only sure facts are that at the end of the session there was a written confession, and that Whitmore had not been beaten. There are, however, several possibilities that may explain how an utterly innocent person gave the complete details of the crime, down to naming the lubricant (Noxzema), that he used to facilitate the rapes.

One is that the detectives prompted the confession. Leading questions can bring out the desired information, and police interrogators under severe pressure to break the case could have resorted to this.

Another is that the interrogators kept at Whitmore to confess, insisting that he supply the details. This is known as the "Yeshov Method" in the Soviet Union, where it was named after a particularly notorious chief of their secret police in the 1930s. [2] Following this method, the suspect is presumed guilty, and the only problem is for him to make an acceptable confession. It's not necessary to beat him, only to keep at him relentlessly, telling him that the only way he can satisfy the interrogator is to confess fully and sincerely. If the confession doesn't please the interrogator, he tells the suspect that he's being "uncooperative," or "insincere." Sooner or later, perhaps with a little prompting, the suspect will produce what the interrogator desires of him.

Part of the aftermath of the Whitmore Affair was that the prosecutors in New York dropped the charges in six other murder cases during the following years. All of the suspects had confessed, but the reputation of the New York City Police Department led to close scrutiny of these confessions and the manner in which they'd been obtained.

196

Main-line police administrators denied the allegations, insisting that their suspects confessed because of a deeply-seated guilt that needed to be relieved, or a clever persistence in exposing the discrepancies in the suspect's story. This was the view expressed by one high official of the New York City Police Department.3 This officer claimed that he simply took down whatever statement the suspect was willing to make, and interviewed him about it the next day, after gathering more information to explore possible discrepancies. The police took down another statement during this second session, and compared it with the previous one. Another session the following day would produce another statement for the police to scrutinize in their search for the truth. The officers would gradually winnow the truth out of the suspect, no matter how unwilling he was to provide it, because they would overwhelm him with their moral and intellectual superiority. This high official concluded by stating categorically that the "third degree" did not and never had existed.

This wasn't a new problem for New York. It wasn't a new problem for the nation. In 1931, the Wickersham Commission issued a report on American police which dealt in part with the methods used for obtaining confessions.4 The commission reported that the "third degree" was alive and well in America. The "third degree" was not merely interrogation with verbal brutality, but also included beatings, starving, using tear gas and chloroform, administering scopolamine, and even lifting the suspect by a rope attached to his genitals.

THE EVANS-CHRISTIE CASE

The problem isn't only with American police. Despite the common stereotypes, American police officers are not inexcusable brutes while foreign police are gentlemen.

The British police have an excellent reputation world-wide. Their pioneering of scientific crime detection in real-life contrast to the deductive and fictional Sherlock Holmes established their standing before the turn of the century. Each year American tourists return suitably impressed by the civilized manner of the British Bobbies, which stands out against their experiences with American "cops." This sterling reputation has been only slightly tarnished by the recent corruption scandals, and it's easy to believe that the British police are basically clean and competent.

This gentlemanly bearing, however, sometimes masks some sinister tendencies. About forty years ago, a man named John Christie murdered seven women and one baby over a period of several years, before the term "serial murderer" came into common use. Despite Christie's raping the dead bodies, the crimes committed are not the worst aspects of the case. The fair-minded officers from Scotland Yard forced a confession out of the wrong man, Timothy Evans, which led to his being convicted and hanged.5

John Christie led a mixed life. A WWI veteran, he also had a record of living off the earnings of a prostitute and of stealing a clergyman's car before settling down to get married. Amazingly, this man was able to become a London Reserve Police Constable in 1939. This was a full-time, paid position, and he held it until he resigned at the end of 1943. At the time he left the police, he'd already started on his second career as a serial murderer. He got a regular job to pay the bills, and continued to murder women.

In 1948, Evans and his pregnant wife moved in upstairs from Christie at 10 Rillington Place,

London. Baby Geraldine was born that year, and on Tuesday, November 8, 1949, Christie murdered Mrs. Evans. Mrs. Evans had become pregnant again, and Christie had offered to give her an abortion.6 When he came to her apartment, there was a struggle, Christie pummeled and strangled Mrs. Evans, and raped her as she died. The details aren't clear because Christie eventually gave several different versions of what happened. What is known is that Mrs. Christie was in the downstairs apartment while this was happening, totally unaware. Evans himself returned from work in the late afternoon, having been told by his wife that she was planning to have Christie abort her. Christie announced to him that the abortion had failed, killing his wife. Evans was dull-normal in intelligence, and Christie found it easy to manipulate him. Evans helped Christie move his wife's body into an unoccupied apartment, pending final disposal. 7

The following day, Christie told Evans that, as he was unable to care for the baby, he (Christie) would arrange to have it adopted by a couple he knew. Christie waited until the next day, when Evans was away from home, and strangled the baby with a necktie. By coincidence, Evans got fired from his job that day, and Christie was able to use this to persuade Evans to abandon the household. Evans also sold his furniture, at Christie's suggestion.

Evans went to Wales, to stay with an uncle and aunt, whom he told his wife and daughter were with relatives in Brighton. Some days later, on November 30th, Evans went to the police station and confessed to having put his wife "down the drain."8 Unfortunately Evans was both dull-witted and a chronic liar, which is one reason he'd gotten fired. He dictated a strange and fantastic statement to the police, which could only have aroused more suspicion than it dissipated. Under questioning, he gave another, contradictory statement, which inflamed suspicions further. Christie was no help when the police arrived at 10 Rillington Place. He told them that Evans had argued repeatedly with his wife, and that his wife had said that she was going to seek an abortion somewhere else in London.

After a search, police officers found the wife's and baby's bodies in the wash-house in the yard. This cast a very grave light on the case, and resulted in Evans' being brought back to London from Wales.[9] The events at the Notting Hill Police Station during the night of December 2 and 3 are not documented, except in two confessions which the police took from Evans. An extra hazard which worked against Evans was that Christie, who was in a position to substantiate Evans' innocence, chose not to for excellent reasons of his own.

For legitimate and easily understandable reasons, explained elsewhere in this book, interrogations take place in private. This also provides an aura of secrecy which makes subsequent investigations into the conduct of an interrogation very difficult. In many instances, there have been conflicting versions of what took place behind closed doors, and this has sometimes resulted in confessions' being thrown out of court. In the case of Evans, the conclusion's fairly clear. Evans was innocent because it turned out that Christie had committed the crimes. This was documented a couple of years later when Christie was tried and convicted for them. Another important consideration is the extreme statistical improbability of two sex murderers living in the same house at the same time and each acting independently of the other.

The internal evidence in police documents shows that Evans was under interrogation for much longer than they claimed.10 Although by the official account, the interrogation was over by 11:15 P.M., Evans later claimed that they were up until five the next morning. The length of the confessions suggests that it would not have been possible to take them down and read them back to him in the time claimed by the detectives who conducted the interrogation. These discrepancies aren't surprising, as one British jurist noted that the British police always claim that their behavior is correct and above reproach.11

While there was no evidence that the British police used physical torture on Evans or any other suspect, psychological pressure was kept very high. Experience with other examples of psychological pressure, such as the Inquisition, forced conversions, etc., shows that if subjected to enough pressure for a long enough time, almost anyone will confess to almost anything. Some of the tactics used by the British police were endless repeating of the same questions, bluffing claims to have all of the evidence in hand, assuring the suspect that a clean confession will make him feel more comfortable, etc. According to Lord Justice Devlin, who conducted an inquiry into the police, the main problem is not the purposeful frame-up of an innocent person, but excessive zeal in pursuing the case against someone they feel to be guilty.12

Evans was especially vulnerable to the sort of psychological manipulation meted out by police interrogators because he'd already been horrified and manipulated by Christie, upon the death of Mrs. Evans. His anxiety over the death of his wife and the fate of his daughter (he thought she'd been adopted by a couple lined up by Christie) combined to put him on edge. The worry and guilt over having helped, even tangentially, to dispose of his wife's body fueled the anxiety. The police aided the process by keeping

Evans in the dark, not informing him of the progress of the case against him, nor telling him why when they took him back to London to the Notting Hill police station. Evans was not too bright, and marginally able to take care of himself in Twentieth-Century society. He was utterly lost when dropped into the hopper of the criminal justice system. Although Evans was a chronic liar, he was putty in the hands of professional flim-flam artists, as the police interrogators were. The length of the interrogation, taking all night, taxed his endurance, and fatigue certainly dulled his judgment.

The net result was that Evans was very suggestible. He accepted whatever the police interrogators told him must have happened. In the peculiar dependency relationship that builds up between the interrogator and the subject, Evans must have developed a desire to please, as has been noted in other subjects given the same treatment.

There's an important similarity between Evans, the British suspect, and Whitmore, the American. Both were poorly educated, and despite a certain amount of "street-smarts," did not truly appreciate their rights, and were not quick-witted enough to resist the pressure of the professional police interrogators.

The Evans case was not the only one in recent British history in which the police obtained confessions which later proved to be false.[13] In others, the police persuaded suspects, some of whom were not too bright, that it was in their best interests to confess.

This sort of happening is an ever-present danger to an interrogator. A desire to succeed, possibly because of simple ambition or because of intense pressure to clear the case, can lead a police interrogator to draw false conclusions, and to enter into a shared delusion with his subject. Political and secret policemen, in many instances not under the constraints of the civil police, commit even greater abuses. In other cases, such as unofficial investigations by private agents, there are no safeguards at all, especially when there's no overt misconduct to investigate.

Pre-employment interviews are occasions for great abuses, and they occur routinely. If a technical device such as the polygraph or voice stress analyzer is part of the process, abuses are guaranteed. This is because these devices are not all-out indicators of deception, but require analysis for a conclusion. This leaves it open to the operator, who is usually influenced by extraneous factors.

All told, interrogation's a chancy tool. In the hands of a dedicated and honest expert, the chances are good that the results will be worthwhile. If, however, the expert is mistaken in his belief, and yet attacks the subject with the same zeal as he would someone truly guilty, the chances for a miscarriage of justice increase proportionately.

Sources

1. *The Mugging,* Morton Hunt, New York, Signet Books, 1972, pp. 109-110.

2. *Battle For The Mind,* William Sargant, Garden City, New York, 1957, p. 213. Yeshov, or "Yezhov," was an especially brutal person who was also known for his mass round-ups during the "purge trial" period. These were called "Yezhovschina" in his honor. Yezhov eventually became too much even for Stalin, who disposed of him in the fashion customary for secret police chiefs at the time, and installed

Lavrenti Beria in his place. Some idea of Yezhov's caliber is evident from the commonly-held view at the time that Beria was a "liberal" and would "professionalize" the NKVD.

3. *The Mugging,* pp. 105-106.

4. *Techniques of Persuasion,* J.A.C. Brown, Baltimore, Maryland, Penguin Books, 1963, pp. 251-252.

5. *Ten Rillington Place,* Ludovic Kennedy, New York, Simon and Schuster, 1961. This book relates the entire story, how Christie killed his victims, and how Timothy Evans, his tenant, was blamed and hanged for two of the murders, and Christie's final confrontation with the criminal justice system.

6. *Ibid.,* pp. 60-63.

7. *Ibid.,* p. 66.

8. *Ibid.,* pp. 83-85.

9. *Ibid.,* p. 97.

10. *Ibid.,* pp. 101-102.

11. *Ibid.,* p. 103.

12. *Ibid.,* p. 114.

13. *Ibid.,* pp. 100-101, and pp. 115-116.

HOW TO SURVIVE INTERROGATION

IS RESISTANCE POSSIBLE?

At first sight, it would seem that when the interrogators have ample time and resources, nobody can possibly resist them indefinitely. In principle this is true, but in principle only. One obvious fact is that not all interrogators have enough time or resources to do the job. Investigators on both sides of the iron curtain usually have to cope with heavy caseloads. Very few cases are so important that they rate a "drop everything" treatment. In the case of many prisoners of war, their very number precludes any intensive effort. The attempts made by the interrogators must be quick, because they can't waste much time on any individual.

They also sometimes work under conditions that don't favor intensive interrogation. When the law prevents holding a suspect incommunicado, the interrogator is deprived of the opportunity to deepen the subject's feeling of isolation. If the suspect's entitled to have a lawyer present to advise him, all hope of producing emotional isolation goes down the tubes.

Prisoners of war often have the advantage of numbers. There usually are too many of them to allow a separate facility for each one. Only specially selected captives, such as pilots, are likely to be given special and intensive treatment. For most soldier-captives, this means that they have the company of their companions to guide and to sustain them.

In some low-key situations, such as when applying for employment, the interrogator doesn't have the same "hold" over his subject as the police do. He cannot prevent the subject from leaving if he so wishes, for example. He also can't keep him from going to the toilet or taking a break for lunch.

Interrogators also make mistakes. Some of them are complacent. Others are simply incompetent. They may misjudge a subject, and not make intensive enough effort to "break" him. In certain extreme situations, the subject may become exhausted enough to endanger his life, and a clumsy interrogator may thusly lose him forever.

Resistance is possible. It's partly luck, if the situation's such that the interrogator can't devote his full attention to the subject. It's also having a working knowledge of what's possible and what's not. A realistic set of expectations is better than the ignorance with which many unfortunate subjects are dragged into interrogation.

The foregoing chapters have given you a good grounding in the principles of and reasons for the various interrogation techniques. Knowing how the process works is the first step in defending yourself if ever you're the subject.

KNOW YOURSELF

You have to be honest in appraising your strengths and weaknesses. Just as an interrogator will tailor his tactics according to the sort of subject before him, so you must adopt methods that work for you.

Ask yourself some important questions:

Are you fast on your feet, mentally? Can you think fast, and come up with the right answers most of the time?

How's your resistance to psychological pressure? Do you feel a need to speak up to fill periods of silence?

In other interviews, such as when applying for a job, have you usually spoken too much, volunteering information that was unneeded? Do you think you can learn to control this?

Can you control your emotions? Can you reply to an accusation without showing either fright or anger?

Do you have a strong need to be liked? Does this affect your relations with people you hardly know? Does it leave you open to emotional bullying by an interrogator?

Can you withstand the emotional attrition of an interrogation away from friends and family?

Do you have powerful friends who can bail you out of trouble?

It's impossible to lay out every step for every type of personality. What we can do here is to examine various tactics that work in these situations. Keep in mind that the great majority of interviews and interrogations that take place are not police matters, but they can still affect your life. When applying for a job, for example, you can expect an interrogation. The tactics have to vary with the situation. In some instances, it's possible to be defiant. In others, playing the game and showing discretion is best. We can also try to set up some mental preparation.

One valuable aid to prepare you for resisting interrogation is the rehearsal. If you have a friend who has the same interests, you can practice interrogating each other. The first step is to set up a scenario in which you might find yourself. The situation should be true-to-life, not pure imagination. Don't try to imagine yourself being investigated on suspicion of having murdered your wife if you're not married. The reason the scenario should be realistic is that a totally imaginary situation won't evoke the same intensity of emotion.

Important to learning how to survive interrogation is the critique. Your buddy should observe you carefully and after the session tell you whether he thought you did adequately. Even better is a third person, who can be a non-participating observer during the sessions. He can observe whether the person acting as the subject was credible, showed excessive nervousness, or gave anything away unnecessarily.

Another valuable preparation is to learn and practice relaxation techniques well before you anticipate an interrogation. You may already be practicing them as a way to cope with the stress of life.

The basic technique is learning to relax selectively the muscle groups in the body. Starting with the toes and progressing up to the head, it's possible to reduce tension and in so doing lower the pulse, blood pressure, and respiration rates. This can help you relax and sleep when you're left alone. It can also help you reduce tension during the interrogation.

WHEN THE MOMENT COMES

The first step is to appraise your situation and estimate your chances. What is the problem? What charges and what consequences face you? The matter can be trivial, such as missing petty cash at the company where you work. It might be critical, as in the case of a spy trying to evade the secret police. The circumstances will have a lot to do with whether you play dumb or try to "stand up for your rights."

The Cover Story

You should have your "cover story" prepared. This may be an explanation of your recent actions or whereabouts or it may be a life history. The basic principle operating is that minor details can be as important as the main threads of the story. This means you have to go through the unglamorous work of memorizing details and more details, but the details can trip you up.

Sometimes it's very simple. An explanation of why you were found in the company office after working hours will get you off the hook if it's convincing. Sometimes it can be more complex, covering a greater period of time and explaining away a lot more actions.

Let's say that you claim to have made a trip to a certain city on a certain date. The interrogator asks you about your mode of travel. You answer that you flew, and even have a cancelled airline ticket to prove it. The interrogator then asks you how you got from the airport to your destination. You'd better have this part down pat! If you claim to have taken a cab, do you know for certain that the cabs were not on strike that day? If you rented a car, which car rental company did you use? Do you know for sure that they have an office in that city? If your answer doesn't satisfy the interrogator, he may dig more deeply into your story, because a cancelled air ticket doesn't prove that you were the passenger.

Imagine another situation. You claim to have lived in Paris during the last two years, giving an address on the Rue St. Dominique. Can you spell it? Can you tell the interrogator if the Rue St. Dominique is on the left bank or the right bank? Can you walk to the university without taking a bus? If not, what bus line do you take? When you step out of your "pension" and turn to the left, do you pass the Ministry of Health or the Minstry of Defense? What's the name of the nearest subway station? What's the fare on the Paris subway? Better know the answers the first time, because the consolation prize may be a firing squad.

One cover story to avoid is the hoary old technique of a "story within a story."[1] This requires having an alternative explanation prepared, one that is derogatory to yourself and which supposedly will therefore be more believable. An example is that of the burglar caught inside an apartment building corridor, but not actually breaking into a residence. Not wanting to admit that he was looking for a suitable apartment to burgle, he tells the person who catches him: "Please don't make a fuss about this. Her husband would kill me if he found out." The reference to adultery makes him look slightly ridiculous, and his excuse for wanting the affair quietly forgotten is reasonable. The problem with this sort of trick is that it's an old one, and to the experienced police officer or interrogator it's a sure sign of sophisticated deception. This is why the story within a story is a tool to use with great discretion. It won't get you very far except with people who have never heard of it.

Sizing Up Your Interrogator

Equally important is your interrogator. You must make an effort to appraise him, to "size him up," as soon as possible. The unfortunate fact about this is that you'll have to do it almost entirely by observation, as it's unlikely that your interrogator will answer questions about himself. Be watchful; the sooner you figure him out, the sooner you'll be able to plan your tactics. Also be watchful for tactical errors which you may exploit. You need all the help you can get and taking advantage of the interrogator's mistakes can give you an edge.

What appearance does he present? Is he a sharp dresser, one who might be trying to impress you with his "professional" appearance and demeanor? If so, you've got the weak point right at hand, and can "kid him along," playing to his vanity.

What about his manner? Does he storm into the room, trying to frighten you? Does he seem to be playing "macho man" to cover a lack of knowledge or preparation?

Many interrogators try to establish "rapport," as we've seen. Some of them restrain themselves to simply getting the subject to talk, but others become saccharin-friendly. Some will try immediately to get on a first-name basis with you. The New York cops are very pushy about this, asking immediately, "What do your friends call you?" Your answer will depend on what posture you've decided to take. You may answer docilely, or start the confrontation by informing the interrogator right out that he's not your friend. If you do so, be prepared to back it up, because this means crossing the Rubicon, and there's no turning back.

Is he trying to play "buddy-buddy" with you? Does he show too much positive emotion for the situation? If so, it's a clumsy attempt to make friends with you, and being aware of this enables you to gain control of the situation. You can pretend to accept his affability and lead him to believe that he's "conned" you into lowering your guard. Feed him your story and see how well he accepts it.

Another approach is the "silent treatment." In our culture, people normally talk to fill gaps, and usually don't tolerate long periods of silence. Many can't stand the sound of silence at all, and chronically play the radio or use another means of filling in the silence. The "silent treatment" also takes advantage of the psychological fact that speaking is a way of reducing emotional tension. Someone accused of a crime, and kept in suspense waiting the interrogator's attention, will feel compelled to say something. If the interrogator pretends to ignore the subject, he may become careless in what he says.

A very common and very old trick is the use of two interrogators, one of whom is hostile and threatening, and the other is friendly and caring. This is the technique known as "good guy-bad guy," or "Mutt and Jeff," and is a variant of the "blow hot and cold" technique. This is one of the "oldest tricks in the book" and yet police still use it because there's a new generation that hasn't heard of it yet.

The countermeasure to this is equally simple. Act properly fearful of the "tough guy," and when he leaves the room say to the "good guy" in a confiding manner: "What am I gonna do? I really didn't do it, but how do I get that guy to believe me?"

It's important to remember, however, that the interrogator doesn't "like" or "dislike" you. He's a professional, just doing his job. He may show approval or anger as a technique for manipulating you, but as long as you remember that his emotions are faked, you'll keep yourself on an even keel. Don't make the mistake of starting to react emotionally to him.

Monitor your mental and physical state. Try to be aware of when you're becoming exhausted. Your mind will begin to play tricks on you and you'll start to feel emotions you can't explain.

After a long interrogation, you may find that, in spite of yourself, you crave the interrogator's approval, and try to say and do things to please him. This is a sure sign that you're losing control of yourself. If the stakes are high enough, it's worth taking drastic measures to interrupt the interrogation. Complain of a pain in the center of your chest. This may get you a visit from a doctor or a trip to the hospital. With a little luck, you can take a few hours' rest.

One valuable tactic is to control the pace of the interrogation. Don't let the interrogator rush you or get you rattled. There are several simple tricks for slowing down the pace:

Light a cigarette. If you still have your pack, take advantage of the tactical error that the interrogator's made. Take a puff before answering every question.

Silently count to five before answering every question.

If you normally bite your nails, keep a finger in your mouth part of the time. Keep a hand up near your mouth as you speak.

Ask for a drink.

Ask to visit the toilet.

Cough.

Stop between sentences, or interrupt yourself in the middle of a sentence. This works especially well when replying to simple questions. If asked your address, start to answer, pause, look at the ceiling, and then give the rest of the address.

Use relaxation techniques. Don't try to hide this. Shift around, relax your muscles, and when, inevitably, the interrogator asks what you're doing, tell him outright that you're using relaxation techniques. He'll immediately jump on this to try to browbeat you, asking you why you're so tense. The implication is that if you were innocent, you'd have nothing to worry about. You simply reply that this sort of interrogation would make anyone nervous, and that you're trying to relax from the strain

DIRECT COUNTERMEASURES

It helps to know the interrogator's ploys and to develop tactics for dealing with them. There are many tricks that interrogators use in verbal sparring to keep their subjects off-balance.

The first ploy to anticipate and counteract is the investigator's attempt to make you relax so that he can catch you off-guard. Interrogators often start off discussing a neutral subject, such as the weather or sports. The next topic might be an attempt to find a common bond. A question about your hobbies is harmless in itself, but it can lead to the interrogator's telling you that he has the same hobby. If he says so, it's probably true, and you can spend several minutes discussing it. If you relax too much while discussing something enjoyable, you may be caught unaware later.

Similarly, you have to be aware of the variations on the "salami-slicing" technique. One is the "Have you ever stolen a cookie" game.2 This is an attempt to make you admit guilt by stages, by asking you if you've ever committed a minor offense, and gradually

214

asking about more serious ones. The interrogator may lay in comments such as: "You probably have. Everybody's done it at one time or other."

Resisting this technique without appearing openly defiant requires some self-control. Keep hold of your temper and say pleasantly, "Just because I stole a cookie years ago doesn't mean that I did this now."

The technique of trying to take the wind out of your sails, which we covered in the "Tactics" session, is a common one, and it gives you an opportunity to disrupt the pace of the interrogation, and throw your opponent off his rhythm. When the interrogator starts his recitation of the possible alibis you might produce, interrupt him to object:

INTERROGATOR: "I know you're probably going to tell me that you weren't even in town that day, but..."

YOU: "So what! Is it a crime to be in town? To be out of town? What's this got to do with anything, anyway?"

This is taking a very strong tone, and it might be better to try a softer approach in order not to seem a wise guy:

INTERROGATOR: "You're probably going to tell me that you stayed home alone, or went out for a walk by yourself..."

YOU: "If I do, are your going to call me a liar? Do you really believe I'm going to sit here and lie to you? Is that what you think of me?"

Some interrogators don't ask questions directly. They'll try to prompt you by repeating a word from the last sentence you spoke:

"I came home directly. I think it was about midnight."

"Think?"

Against such a tactic, simply stand your ground without giving in to the pressure to speak out to justify yourself further. In this case, a simple "yes" will do perfectly. If the interrogator wants more, let him ask for it. Going into a long monolog to justify why your thinking is correct will simply get you in deeper and give him more points to question.

There's one situation in which you'll be extremely vulnerable to this sort of tactic. When applying for employment, the normal values are reversed. The burden of proof is upon the applicant, or so the interviewer would have them believe. To get the job, the applicant goes through steps that a felony suspect would never have to take. Filling out the application can be a serious chore. Some of them ask for personal details that are truly none of the interviewer's business. You don't have to answer any question, of course, but he doesn't have to employ you, either.

There is a tactful and inoffensive way to answer an interviewer's probing question, or to deal with his masked questions. If an interviewer tries repeating a single word to you, as discussed above, answer as simply as you can. If he expresses doubt, by a raised eyebrow or other non-verbal technique, ignore it. You'll feel the pressure to answer and justify yourself because you want the job. If you must substantiate your answer, the best way to do so is to tell the interviewer that the facts of your employment history support what you claim, and that he can easily check this out by contacting former employers.

This is an excellent tactic, and many applicants use it as a bluff. They know that personnel interviewers are usually either overworked or lazy, and will not take the extra step of verifying an applicant's employment history.

Be wary of the surreptitious interrogation. This is a very common tactic and the reason that it's not well-documented is that few people are aware that it's being practiced on them, especially if it's not in a criminal setting. We find this type of interrogation common in pre-employment screening. The reason for this tactic is that interviewers know that job applicants aren't going to admit derogatory facts gratuitously during a formal interview. If there's a question relating to something that the interviewer can check, most people will play it safe and be honest. They know intuitively that lying will count heavily against them when discovered.

One possible topic is drug use, common in many occupations nowadays. This is a probing personal question, but it's justifiable in the eyes of employers because it relates to illegal acts. It's hard to cover up an arrest for a drug-related offense, but without an arrest record, it's quite possible to deny drug use. We know this, and so does the interviewer. He knows that a "friendly" and "informal" talk might bring this out.

This sort of interrogation happens after the formal one. The interrogator says that it's time for a break, or for lunch, and invites you to accompany him. The odds are that this encounter will take place where alcoholic drinks are available. This is reason for extra caution.

Getting sloshed is, of course, a "no-no," but so is drinking too eagerly. It's hard to say what is excessive in drinking, because that depends on the person doing the interviewing.[3] It's also vital to know your limit, and not trangress it, because you may find your judgment affected, your inhibitions dulled, and this may lead you to say too much.

In this setting, you have to lie on two levels:

It's necessary to present an acceptable picture of yourself, one that will persuade the interviewer that you're worthy of the job.

It's also necessary to avoid letting on that you've figured out what's happening. You don't want to bruise his ego, for one, by making it appear that he was clumsy enough for you to find him out. You also want to continue to appear unknowing to give credence to what you say during this session.

The interviewer will tend to ramble on about different topics. If the opportunity presents itself to admit something derogatory, don't be too reluctant. The key is admitting derogatory information that's within the range of normal behavior. This will make it seem that you're being candid. Of course, deny anything serious, but make the denial plausible. Interviewers can, in this setting and others, use the salami-slicing technique with devastating effect on anyone who doesn't have good judgment and a clear idea of when to dig in his heels.

Let's look at a hypothetical conversation:

INTERVIEWER: "Cigarette?"

YOU: "No, thanks, I don't smoke."

INTERVIEWER: "I have a neighbor who uses cocaine. Nice guy, and in fact his wife is my wife's best friend. You know anybody who uses coke?" (Watch out: here it comes!)

218

YOU: "Oh yes, a few people I know use it, and my neighbor's business partner does cocaine." (This was a good answer. It provides a credible and non-damaging admission without going overboard in volunteering a denial that you use it. Keep playing it cool.)

INTERVIEWER: "You ever use it?"

YOU: "No. A friend offered some to me a couple of years ago, but I was scared to try it. I've seen what it can do." (That's good, too. A straight denial without laying it on too much.)

INTERVIEWER: "Drink much?" (He's probing again, but into a slightly less dangerous area. Still, be careful.)

YOU: "Only like this, a beer or two with friends." (A good answer. Saying "with friends" isn't exactly what you meant, because the interviewer is definitely not a friend, but he'll be pleased. It shows that you've let your guard down somewhat.)

This is far enough with this example. Handling this sort of post-interviewing attempt isn't difficult, as long as the interviewer is interested in only illegal and anti-social behavior. One who starts discussing politics is very dangerous because it's impossible to out-guess him unless you already know him or know about him. An interviewer may express some way-out political ideas to test you. Unfortunately, you may not know if he's sincere. You don't know whether to pretend to agree with him or not, because he might simply be saying it to trap you.

Interviewers, especially the ones trying to be clever, can be very devious. One who asks you if you like

Gore Vidal's novels, for example, might be probing your attitude towards homosexuality because Vidal is a self-admitted homosexual author. Other novelists, such as Ayn Rand and Arthur Miller, have taken prominent political stands, and admitting that you've read their works might be interpreted that you approve of their politics. This reasoning seems far-fetched, but there are many people who think this way. They can be dangerous to you if they ever have some hold on you, such as the power to withhold employment.

The discussion might touch on other matters, such as capital punishment, sex, adultery, previous experiences with employers, etc. Without knowing exactly what he's seeking, the best course is to pretend to be middle-of-the road in social and political attitudes. Most businesses want stable people who work within the "system" and won't rock the boat. Unless the situation is such that you know that the company needs non-conformists with unusual and inquiring minds, pretending mediocrity will be best.

In an extreme situation, you may become a prisoner of war. This is one of the most unhappy situations you can face, but it can vary a lot, depending on the war and your role in it. You may be captured in good health, or wounded. Your relationship to your captors will often determine the treatment you receive. If you're a simple infantryman, you blend in with many others. If you're surviving aircrew, and your captors have had their cities attacked and civilians killed, don't expect them to hold a charitable attitude towards you. You'll probably be selected for "special treatment," which can be rigorous.

Your captors will, of course, determine the sort of treatment you get. If they're members of a nation that follows the Geneva Convention's rules for dealing with prisoners of war, you may get good treatment. This isn't always true, however. The Germans usually observed the provisions of the Geneva Convention, but in 1944, when over 50 prisoners escaped from one of their POW camps, Hitler ordered that they be shot upon recapture, and they were.

In certain instances, your captors may have an attitude of profound contempt for you because you allowed yourself to be captured. This is the attitude that the Japanese held towards Allied POWs during WWII, because their code was not to be taken alive. Dying for the Emperor was a duty, and in fact few Japanese fighting men were taken prisoner. If you're captured by people with this attitude, expect to be treated worse than an animal, because they'll see you as contemptible and totally undeserving of respect.

Communist captors see political value in POWs, and make varying efforts to obtain anti-war statements from them. The armed services have tried to counter this by establishing a code of conduct for American fighting men, which we examined earlier. The viewpoint of the government is that American servicemen captured should make an effort to remain cohesive units, and to abide by their principles.[4]

The manual contains many practical tips to help the serviceman resist interrogation and other efforts to subvert his loyalty. There's supreme reliance upon group spirit, and maintaining a command structure. Each camp must have a senior officer, and he appoints subordinates to whom he delegates duties. Prisoners are still American servicemen, and captivity doesn't release them from the obligations of duty.

221

Generally, POWs who remain in groups have a much better chance of resisting than those who are kept isolated. In groups, they usually get "new blood" as additional captives swell their ranks. These newcomers bring news from home, and news about the war. They may even have information on the prospects for release. Some may be specially-trained intelligence operatives who let themselves be captured on purpose so that they might stiffen the morale of the POWs.

Keeping together, the group can resist enemy tactics more readily. The combination of emotional sustenance and peer pressure work to produce conformity to group goals. POWs can exchange information about enemy interrogation tactics, and build each other's morale. They can also resist efforts to split individuals from their groups. Some captors may try to encourage collaboration by giving special privileges. This usually isn't anything drastic, as they start with the "salami-slicing" technique. A slight favor brings a small reward, and it's easy to argue that it does no harm. This draws the collaborating POW closer, and at some point he starts to realize that he's cooperating more than he'd intended.

The isolated POW is in an almost hopeless situation. Without fellow POWs to sustain his morale, he's extremely vulnerable. The enemy, by controlling the news he gets, can try to make him believe anything. If they tell him that the war is over, but that his country has abandoned him, he may easily believe it. Another plausible story is; "They don't know we've got you. They think you were killed in the crash." This can shift his perspective and convince him that keeping silent doesn't matter anymore.

Isolation is devastating. Whatever indoctrination the POW received during training, his superiors are not there to sustain him. The people who wrote the POW Code of Conduct are safe at home. This can't be very reassuring to the isolated POW.

In such a case, the POW has nothing but his internal resources to sustain him. The captors have absolute power over him. The outcome depends partly on what sort of personality type he has. Although men are not dogs, the basic mechanism of the nervous system is similar in both, and some types are more resistant to pressure and stress than others.

OPTIMISM

It would be a mistake to end this chapter on a terrifyingly pessimistic note. Although interrogation and indoctrination techniques are effective, and with enough effort anyone can be "broken" — if he survives — this doesn't happen as often as the interrogators wish. Individual incompetence and adverse circumstances often combine to defeat the interrogator. The frightening and absolute effectiveness of O'Brien, the interrogator in George Orwell's *1984*, is fiction. No totalitarian regime has the resources to pursue every case of political deviation so relentlessly. In real life, people have withstood interrogation in the worst circumstances. Preparedness and luck were decisive.

Sources

1. *Liar's Manual*, Roland Baker, Chicago, Illinois, Nelson-Hall, Publishers, 1983, pp. 38-42.

2. *The Gentle Art of Interviewing and Interrogation*, Robert F. Royal and Steven R. Schutt, Englewood Cliffs, New Jersey, Prentice-Hall, 1976, pp. 143-144.

3. It's also possible to be condemned for not drinking: *Liar's Manual*, p. 194.

4. *Prisoner of War Resistance*, FM 21-78. Commercially reprinted by Paladin Press, Boulder, Colorado.

FUTURE PROSPECTS

The future of interrogation is open to speculation, as is the future of almost anything else. However, there's more room for doubt here because of the interlocking factors which affect the status of interrogation. Instead of taking the giant step of making predictions, let's instead look at the possible progress in each field which can affect interrogation. This makes for a fascinating study, but one which we'll have to deal with quickly, since so much is yet unknown and unpredictable.

INTERROGATION TACTICS

There are not likely to be any new tactics discovered. There are so many "games" and permutations possible, and many of these are already restricted by law. The future of interrogation tactics depends more upon legal developments than on innovations by interrogators. Let us therefore look at possible developments in the law next.

THE LAW

Is there a future for the Fifth Amendment? While it seems sacrilegious even to question this, there are some disturbing possibilities which together may transform the way we think of "civil rights."

One is the pendular swing of attitudes towards law and order. The past three decades have brought increased concern for the rights of the accused, extending to watchful advocacy of the rights of those convicted of crimes. There's a growing feeling that this concern has gone too far. One obvious fact is the prolonged neglect of the victims of crime. They are often lost in the shuffle, and forgotten. The criminal justice system, including the police, prosecutor, and the court, give them brief attention as long as they serve to help capture and convict the offender. Afterwards, they vanish into limbo, abandoned with their hurt.

This has caused a reaction. Not only do we see a start at compensating the victims of crime, but an increased interest in restitution. We also see an increase in retribution, with the return of capital punishment.

One logical development of this trend is repeal of the Fifth Amendment of the Bill of Rights. One "common sense" argument is that if a person's innocent, he has nothing to hide. This is somewhat simple-minded, but we have to consider the exasperation of the people with a criminal justice system in which the deck is stacked decisively in favor of the criminal and against the victim. There's been justifiable rage, for example, at the spectacle of a female rape victim being treated like a slut by the defendant's attorney if she dares to testify at the trial.

If people feel that they are besieged by criminals, they may vote a modification of the Bill of Rights. History has shown that in situations where there's a choice between freedom and security, people will choose security most of the time. Realistically, the defendant's rights are of little concern to most people. Most of us have criminal histories that don't exceed traffic tickets, and don't really care about the Miranda warning. We can't see ourselves in such a situation.

Another approach, this one entirely from "left field," is a change in the perception of the criminal. If we see him as an evil person deserving punishment, we have to be concerned that the punishment fit the crime. If, on the other hand, we perceive him as a deviant needing "adjustment," other criteria apply.

For at least fifty years, there's been a split in penology, a sharp division between those in favor of "custody" and "punishment," and those in favor of "rehabilitation" and "treatment." Decades of experience have shown that rehabilitation has been largely ineffective. The blame for this is mostly because of the methods used. The rehabilitators have had a liberal and humanitarian viewpoint, and have placed their faith in a psychological doctrine based upon the now discredited psychoanalytic viewpoint.

Taking a more practical and utilitarian view, we can propose a new value structure, and a new plan for action:

(1) The criminal has violated the rights of others. He therefore has forfeited his rights.

(2) The main responsibility of the criminal justice system is to protect the rest of society against the criminal.

(3) Any method which is necessary to serve this purpose is therefore legitimate.

Following this line of reasoning, we can see prospects for more vigorous treatment of offenders. To date, nobody's done a study to count the cost of releasing defendants. The criminal released because certain avenues of investigation are barred will go out to victimize more people. Nobody really knows how many. Nobody really knows which affords the greatest good for the greatest number. If there is such a study undertaken in the near future, we may find that the cost of wrongly releasing a guilty person is far greater than the cost of wrongly convicting an innocent one.

With less concern for the rights of the accused, we may find the way to a more efficient administration of justice. There would be more latitude for the introduction of sophisticated technological innovations.

HIGH TECHNOLOGY

A newly-developed instrument can determine if a person's under the influence of certain mind-altering chemicals, and within certain sharp limits, identify the substance. This is the Veritas! Model 100 Analyzer, a comprehensive drug/alcohol detection system.[1] This device is essentially a small, portable, and computerized electro-encephalograph. It picks up and records brain waves, and by observing their pattern, the operator can detect the influence of certain drugs. Each drug, such as alcohol or marijuana, affects the individual's brain wave pattern differently. It's valuable for a polygraph examiner or an interrogator to know if his subject's under the influence of drugs which affect his reactions to stress.

A future prospect is a computerized "truth verifier," or "lie detector" based upon brain wave patterns. Because this sort of test is non-invasive, the legal objections to it can't be very strong. This, at the moment, is only science fiction, but so was space travel fifty years ago.

A more realistic prospect is a computerized "trial." The problems with juries are well-known, especially among those who are in daily contact with the court system. Our judges aren't perfect, either. Although this form of determining guilt or innocence may seem terribly dehumanized, it may be more accurate than using a judge and jury who can be swayed by prejudice.

There may be one or more new "hi-tech" methods devised for telling truth from lies, using unproven physiological symptoms. Based on the history of such devices so far, the outlook is not very bright. However, the need is so great that many people in both the public and private sectors are very receptive to the promise of such a device, and eager to buy one, even if it's untried. A promoter who devises a telescopic device that "reads" retinal patterns on the inside of the eyeball could probably find some customers if he were to promise that it could detect lies. The appeal would be greatly enhanced if the device permitted clandestine use. Scanning a subject without his knowledge would avoid the sticky problems of obtaining consent and of possible lawsuits. The success of the voice analyzers has given a good indication of the possible market.

Less promising is the use of drugs. Experience with psycho-pharmacology has shown that the effects of drugs upon the personality tend to be unpredictable and destructive. There are yet many great mysteries regarding the way in which the brain operates, and finding a chemical which compels a person to tell the truth is in the far future, at best.

Other technological methods such as advanced electroshock techniques and the various forms of brain surgery are equally unpromising at best. They don't work well at "curing" psychiatric patients, and as aids to interrogation they're practically hopeless. Their only possible use is after conviction, as methods of partially incapacitating career criminals. Destruction of parts of their brains, by electricity or by surgery, may dull their intellects enough to make them incompetent to commit crimes. This, therefore, may save the state the expense of prolonged incarceration.

TRENDS

These trends will all affect the future of interrogation. Some trends may continue in the same vein, while others, such as the concern for the arrestee's rights, are likely to see a reversal. Whatever the combination that results, the sure loser is the innocent individual, who is almost defenseless against aggressive intruders into his privacy. The career criminal is likely to continue "getting away with murder."

Sources

1. Manufactured by:
   National Patent Analytical Systems, Inc.
   Expressway Plaza Two
   Roslyn Heights, NY 11577
   Phone: (516) 484-3090

YOU WILL ALSO WANT TO READ: